NORMANDY 1944

the invasion,
the battle,
everyday life

Documentation: Isabelle PAULOU-BOURNIER
Layout: Anne SABLERY

Rémy DESQUESNES
HISTORIAN
DOCTEUR D'ETAT

NORMANDY 1944

the invasion,
the battle,
everyday life

Translated by John Lee

EDITIONS OUEST-FRANCE
MEMORIAL DE CAEN

INVASIONS BEFORE NORMANDY

The United States was just getting into its stride in the mobilization and training of its armies, navies and air forces... They were still only partially trained. The great bulk of the fighting equipment, naval, air, and ground needed for the invasion did not exist. Some of the landing craft were not yet in the blueprint stage... In the summer of 1942 it took a very considerable faith, not to say optimism, to look forward to the day when the potentialities of the United States would be fully developed and the power of the three great Allies could be applied simultaneously and decisively against the European Axis. This attitude of faith was demanded at all superior headquarters. Any expression of defeatism or any failure to push ahead in confidence was instant cause for relief from duty, and all officers knew it.

D.D. Eisenhower

DIEPPE Jubilee

Dieppe. Approching the shore.

There is a too common tendency only to remember the Allied invasion from the Second World War, probably because of the fact that the operation took place along the coasts of France. In a way, between the defeat of June 1940 and the Anglo-American operation in June 1944, there would appear to be in the collective memory a big blank corresponding to the rather hazy period of occupation. The reality, it must be said, is very different. Without any shadow of a doubt, the battle of Normandy may be ranked among the decisive military operations of the Second World War. Even though it did not bring an end to the war, the Allied victory at Falaise came in the wake of a long series of hard-fought battles, and although it took place at a later date, it had nothing to envy other famous names such as El Alamein, Guadalcanal, Kursk or Monte Cassino! In short, like Stalingrad, Falaise was a decisive step on the way to final victory.

The same holds for *Overlord,* codename of the Allied landing in the Channel. Although deliberately placed under the protection of the Almighty, this operation was not due to a miracle of the gods in favour of the Anglo-Saxon strategists, far from it. There was nothing magical about the Normandy landings, and nor were they unique, since this great operation benefited largely from lessons learnt during previous more or less unsuccessful amphibious attempts. It was the result of gropings, approximations, adjustments and successive improvements. Before *Overlord,* there had been, not to mention operations conducted by the Americans in the distant Pacific, the costly disaster at Dieppe, another clumsy assault on the coasts of north Africa, a full-scale dress rehearsal, in July 1943, on the southern coast of Sicily, another two training exercises on the shores of the Italian peninsula, at Salerno and at Anzio. In a word, before playing their sonata to perfection in the Channel, for many long years the Allies had been practising their scales!

These are the combined operations previous to the Normandy expedition that should first be recalled, since it is very true that we can only gain a full grasp of a historical event, whether military or otherwise, by going back to its origins.

Of all the amphibious operations carried out by the Allies on the Western front, Dieppe has a place apart. Occurring roughly midway between the retreat from Dunkirk and the Normandy invasion, *Jubilee* was the first large-scale attempt at direct aggression against the *Wehrmacht* along the shores of France. An operation resting almost exclusively on the shoulders of the Canadian army, impatient to get into combat, Dieppe was a failure that would be exploited by Nazi propaganda to stress the impregnable character of the Atlantic Wall.

A raid, not an invasion

It should be stressed from the outset that, like the daring attack launched by British commandos against the German radar station at Bruneval or against the big dry dock at the port of Saint Nazaire, in March 1942, what is commonly known as the Dieppe invasion was really no more than a large-scale raid. The actual mission, in August 1942, of the 6,000 men, 5,000 of whom belonged to General McNaughton's 1st Canadian Army, was to come ashore along a front about twelve miles wide either side of the seaside resort of Dieppe, to stay on land for the duration of two tides, that is about twelve hours, and to inflict maximum damage on the enemy: destroy the coastal defences, the airfield at Saint-Aubin, a radar station, a power station supplying energy, the port installations at Dieppe, the railways and fuel depots, and seize prisoners and secret documents at the Division command post. Once those objectives had been achieved, the assailants were to withdraw and return to England. As we see, there was no question of a proper landing operation aimed at creating a permanent beachhead along the Channel coast from which to launch subsequent operations against the occupying forces.

A controversial operation

Whilst the assault fleet comprising 250 warships and landing craft was approaching the French coast, in the small hours of August 19 1942, a few Allied units met a German convoy coming down the Channel. A violent confrontation ensued which alerted the defenders on land. All that they had to do then was to pre-

Dieppe. The assault fleet.

Dieppe. Assisting the shipwrecked.

pare a welcoming party for the commando that was about to set foot on land on the beach at Le Puys. Fighting an unequal and hopeless battle, the gallant Canadian detachment was literally mown down by machine-guns hidden in prearranged combat positions. At the other end of the assault area, apart from destroying the shore battery at Varengeville, the attackers, deprived of the support of the tanks stuck on the pebble beach at Dieppe, had to turn back in the face of the vigorous German response. In the centre of the sector of operations, the attack on the beach of Dieppe resulted in almost total failure. The Canadian infantry soldiers were pinned down under murderous enemy fire. In a word, *Jubilee* was an unmitigated disaster, and, except at Berneval and Varengeville, not a single objective had been reached. By evening on August 19, losses were catastrophic: on returning to the quays at Newhaven, more than one man in two was missing and the number of killed alone reached nearly a thousand. Given such carnage for an operation that had hardly lasted 9 hours, what then would it be like on the day the Allies made their big return to the continent? After this brutal experience, the Canadian survivors who, a few days earlier, had been keen to take on the Germans, were now convinced that war is in no way a game and that any battle is a cruel and merciless business.

The lessons of Dieppe

It is true that *Jubilee* remains the bloodiest expedition that the Canadian army had yet embarked upon and the greatest military disaster in the history of that country. However, the Allied command would draw some useful lessons from this costly adventure for future operations, such as the need to carry out an aerial bombing prior to any assault against a fortified coastline, to ensure permanent air cover for the beachhead, to ship across artillery to provide support for the troops on the ground, to maintain the surprise element right up till the last moment, to use paratroops as a diversionary force before launching the seaborne assault, to have an adequate communications network to provide the commanders with fully up-to-date progress reports, to supply better training for the men.... However the main lesson is not there. Although in a way inhuman, without any doubt, Dieppe would provide an answer to the crucial question that the Allied strategists were asking themselves: what were the chances of success of an invasion against a port defended and fortified by the Germans? In showing that any frontal assault against a continental port was heading for certain failure, *Jubilee* would encourage the Allied chiefs of staff to pursue research towards perfecting a revolutionary combined operation enabling a large-scale landing to take place away from the conventional installations of a large port. The Allied operation in north Africa in November 1942 was again launched in the immediate vicinity of large ports (Casablanca, Oran, Alger). It was only eight months later, in Sicily, that the Allies were to attempt for the first time a large-scale landing on open beaches, away from a port. An enormous step forward had thus been taken in the technique of amphibious operations.

Dieppe. A costly business.

NORTH AFRICA Torch

It was on the coasts of north Africa, as Churchill had wished, and not on the shores of the Channel, that the first big Anglo-American landing took place, three months after Dieppe. Codenamed *Torch* (the torch of freedom), and placed under the command of the American General Eisenhower, the operation was the first stage in the British battle plan designed to attack the Axis powers in their more distant conquests.

The first combined Anglo-American operation

Wresting the initiative from the Axis in a secondary theatre of operations, chasing the Italians and Germans out of Africa and keeping the promise made to Stalin in 1942 to open a second front, these were the strategic objectives of *Torch.* The sector chosen for the attack was nearly 950 miles long, stretching from Casablanca to Algiers, that is to say along both the Atlantic and the Mediterranean coasts. Such an over-extended assault front can be explained quite simply by the Allies' refusal to run the risk of finding themselves trapped in the Mediterranean by a possible blockade of the Straits of Gibraltar. Three landings were planned: an exclusively American contingent in the Casablanca area, on Morocco's Atlantic seaboard, and the two others carried out by mixed Anglo-American forces in the region of Oran and Algiers. Once a beachhead had been successfully established, the Allied troops were to march eastwards, join up with Montgomery's army coming from the western border of Egypt, thus gripping the Axis forces in a huge vice.

Landing 100,000 men

Comprising three *Task Forces* (three autonomous naval forces), the Allied armada comprised an assault force (more than 200 warships, including several aircraft-carriers), a protection force for the convoys, a force carrying supplies and a little more than a hundred troop transport ships and landing craft. Setting off from Portland and Norfolk, in Virginia in this month of October 1942, the *Western Task Force* exclusively comprising units belonging to the US Navy, followed the same course as Christopher Columbus in the opposite direction with the *Niña* and the *Pinta,* 450 years before. Heading towards Oran and Algiers, the two other convoys had left from British ports.
In theory, it had been planned to land during the night of November 8 and the following day approximately 35,000 soldiers per sector, that is a total 100,000 men. With a lightly fortified coast such as this, it had been decided that the landing operation would not be preceded by aerial or naval bombardment of the beach

Landing craft mechanized (L.C.M.).

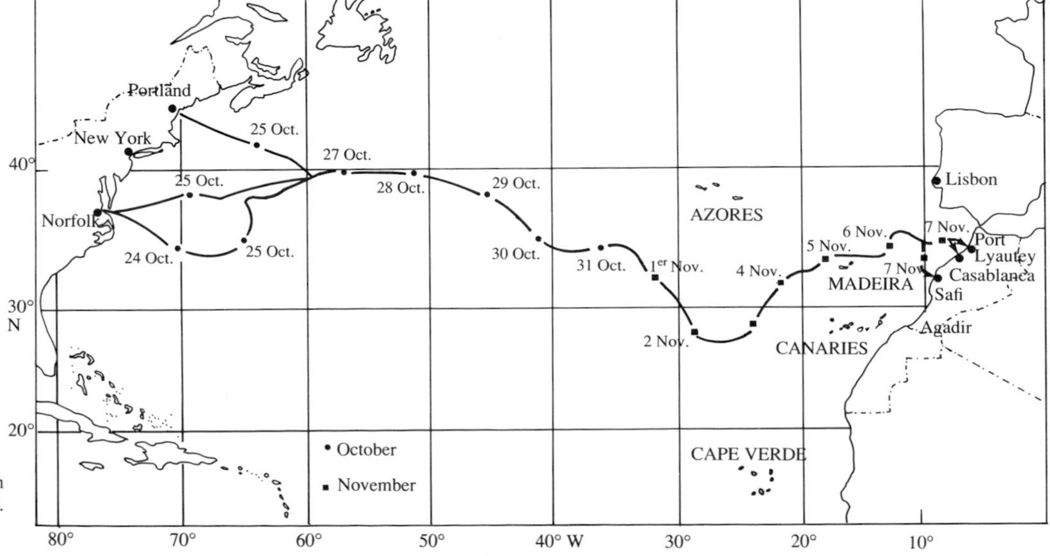

Trajectory covered by the American fleet between October 24 and November 8 1942.

defences. Although a little sluggish, the landing went more or less as planned and once sporadic resistance from the French had been overcome, we may say that by November 10 the Anglo-Americans had control of the entire north-west coast of the African continent, from southern Morocco to the heights of Algiers. Overall, losses in men had been slight, and only about thirty warships, mostly smaller units, had been sunk by torpedoes fired from enemy submarines.

The lessons of *Torch*

As for the Allied commanders, they were under no illusions and perfectly aware that the easy success of *Torch* was due to a whole set of favourable conditions: the absence of coastal fortifications, total surprise, a poor response from the defenders... Some remembered the the Canadian attackers had received a very different welcome three months before in the Channel. In spite of its success, *Torch,* which had progressed infinitely slower than expected, still looked like a match that had been fought without training. On the evening of November 8, for example, in the American sector, only half of the troops had been landed and, due to the violence of the ebb tide, there had been considerable holdups in the unloading of equipment and, consequently, a severe backlog in the units' departure times. To this waste of time, partly due to the inadequate training of the soldiers in the use of large scramble nets hanging down the side of the transport ships into the assault barges, must be added the loss of equipment. Collisions, manoeuvring errors, landing craft coming ashore with the bow door facing out to sea, lowering the ramps of the LCP, LCM or LCV too soon, obliging the soldiers to swim under enemy fire (fortunately not too aggressive here), or flooding the vehicle or tracked engine motors, are attributable to incompetence on the part of the crews. To offset the slowness of the comings and goings between the shore and the ships anchored offshore, the marines tended to overload the landing craft, which sank in the slightest gust of wind in the open sea or in the heavy breakers along the coast. Thus, in some cases, losses of landing craft type vessels exceeded 90 per cent of the numbers engaged! The creation of a special force equipped with pontoons and floating cranes capable of refloating craft that had run aground became necessary for future operations. Similarly, for lack of documents (panoramic aerial photographs with information about the coasts as seen from out to sea, three-dimensional sketches...) and because of the darkness and coastal currents along the African shore, the pilots had great difficulty in locating their landing beaches. The result was a dispersal of the forces,

Opposite page, *Torch.* View of the assault fleet.

the confusion of the different units involved and chaotic unloading (vehicles on one beach with their drivers on another). A further embarrassment was the lack of special LST type ships capable of transporting and unloading armoured vehicles along the beaches at the same time as the assault infantry. During *Torch,* the large majority of the tanks were transported on board conventional ships whose unloading required the prior capture of port facilities, hence, once again, more or less lengthy delays, idle waiting, and lost time. Essential to ensure the success of any amphibious operation, the LSTs, big tank transport ships capable of running aground directly onto the beaches, initially designed by the Americans for their operations in the Pacific, would make their appearance for the first time in the theatre of European operations, in Sicily, in July 1943.

Morocco. Atlantic coast. November 8 1942. *Landing craft.*

Fedala. The Americans come ashore.

" In November 1942, the Allied nations possessed, except for the Gibraltar Fortress, not a single spot of ground in all the region of western Europe, and in the Mediterranean area, nothing west of Malta. Britain's Gibraltar made possible the invasion of northwest Africa. Without it the vital air cover would not have been quickly established on the North African fields... Even several weeks before D-day it became jammed with fighter aircraft. Every inch was taken up by either a Spitfire or a can of gasoline. All this was exposed to the enemy's reconnaissance planes and not even an attempt at camouflage could be made."

D.D. Eisenhower

SICILY Husky

Having chased the Axis out of Africa in May 1943, the objective of the western Allies was now to get a foothold on the continent of Europe through Sicily, restore free navigation in the Mediterranean, eliminate Italy from the war with Germany and get her to change sides. Thanks to *Husky* (codename of the Sicily landing), the Anglo-Americans were hoping both to relieve the Russian front by drawing and holding about twenty German divisions in Italy and to make things easier for the big cross-Channel invasion due around May 1st 1944.

From Licata to Syracuse

Initially, the Allied commanders had planned to carry out a double landing, one on the northern coast, and the other on the south coast, in order to take the Italians and Germans in a pincer movement. As this project went contrary to the sacred principle of concentration of the forces, it was finally abandoned in favour of a single landing in the south-east corner of the island, between the ports of Licata to the west and Syracuse to the east, along a 100 mile front. All this southern corner of the island had the advantage of being within range of permanent cover from Allied fighter planes based in Malta and the airfields of Tunisia. However, although it had big sandy or pebbly beaches, this sector was less suitable for beaching the big landing craft (LST, LCT...) because of the unfavourable gradient of the shore and the fact that, unlike the Pacific, there were no coral reefs off these beaches but instead shallow waters running parallel to the shore. British troops under Montgomery were to land in the eastern sector, on a 40 milefront between Catana and Messina, Bradley's Americans, to the west, on a front of similar length, between Gela and Licata. Between the two assault forces, again placed under the command of General Eisenhower, there stretched a corridor about fifteen miles wide. A year later, a comparable disposition of forces was used in Normandy, but on a front only half that length, due to the more systematic defences.

After their defeat in Tunisia in May 1943, the Germans were expecting an operation in the Mediterranean, "something was in the wind...", wrote US Navy Admiral Samuel Morison, so the Allies set up a deception plan intended to make the Intelligence Services of Admiral Canaris believe that the next expedition would take place in Sardinia or the Peloponnesus. To confirm Hitler's fears, the Allied air forces began a programme of bombing attacks against airfields, roads, bridges and tunnels, railways etc, particularly in Sardinia.

Sicily. Bringing equipment ashore.

301
301

The biggest invasion of the war

Sicily. L.S.T.

For the operation in Sicily, the Allies had gathered together sufficient means to launch a gigantic assault. Never before had an armada been assembled numbering over 3,500 ships of all kinds including 750 warships, or an air fleet of 4,000 British and American units with orders to disable the enemy air power, carry out various transport operations and ensure permanent air cover for the beachhead. Prior to the dropping of two airborne divisions whose mission was to destroy or capture a certain number of nerve centres, the sea-borne invasion took place by moonlight, starting at 3 a.m. on July 10. It involved the landing of 8 infantry divisions, 24,000 vehicles, 1,800 guns and 600 tanks! With a first wave of more than 160,000 men, the initial assault in Sicily remains a record that was never equalled, even in Normandy a year later! From July 11, that is D+1, the Americans (and not for the last time we are tempted to write, now that after *Omaha* we know the rest of the story) were to face a vigorous counter-attack led by German armoured vehicles rushing down the slopes of the hills above the narrow Sicilian beaches. The enemy's plan paid off: a scathing offensive was launched at the critical moment that follows any amphibious operation when the beachhead lacks depth, and before the attacker can muster his entire fighting force. Here, the Americans were all the more vulnerable due to the considerable backlog in unloading operations that had built up because of heavy seas and the presence of sandbanks, which meant that the large LST had to beach much earlier than intended, so far out as made unloading impossible without first setting up a roadway on metal pontoons.

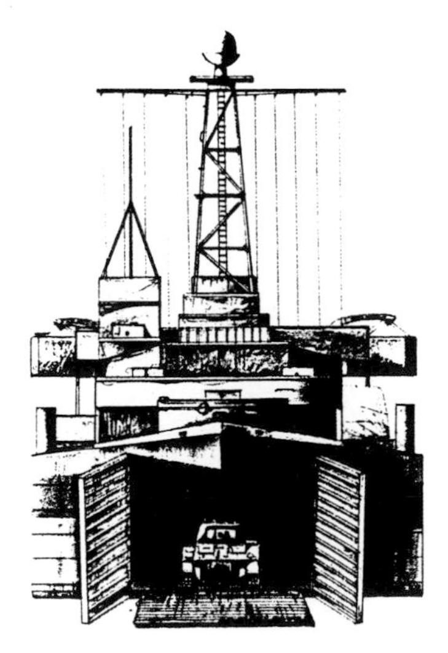

Finally, after many hours of fierce combat, massive intervention of the sea-borne artillery and the fighter bombers saved the day. In spite of their prompt and vigourous reaction, the Germans were unable to throw the Americans back into the sea. After July 1943 the lesson was clear: without air cover from the *Luftwaffe,* any counter-attack launched against the Allies by the *Panzers* was doomed to failure. Once the crisis was over, it remained for the Allies to join up the two assault sectors in a single continuous beachhead enabling wider manoeuvres to be attempted, with the capture of enemy airfields or the construction of air-strips a top priority in order to maintain control in the air and subsequently capture a few large ports (Syracuse, Palermo...).

Husky a precursor of Overlord

With the benefit of the lessons learnt during *Torch* and the experience gained by the Americans in the Pacific against the Japanese, *Husky* was a big step forward in the history of amphibious operations. Only a year had passed since the disaster at Dieppe and eight months since the *Torch* adventure. Indeed it is true to say that Sicily prefigures Normandy more than it is reminiscent of Africa. In both cases, in the Mediterranean and in the Channel, a powerful assault was carried out on open beaches, away from the installations of a large continental port, thanks to an armada of specialised ships (LST, LCT) capable of running directly aground. However, as in June 1944 the Allies were to employ two artificial harbours, it would be more correct to state that *Overlord* was a variation rather than a repetition of the Sicilian experiment. Having said that, if we consider the general organization, the articulation of the various forces engaged, the progress of the operation, the diversionary manoeuvres, the use of air photography, radar, submarines used as marker buoys, amphibious trucks, the commandos and gliders used to transport airborne troops including the 82nd *US Airborne Division* that would later drop over Sainte-Mère-Eglise, or again the names of the commanders (Eisenhower, Montgomery, Bradley, Patton, Ramsay, Hewitt, Tedder...), the obvious conclusion is to draw a parallel between *Husky* and *Overlord.*

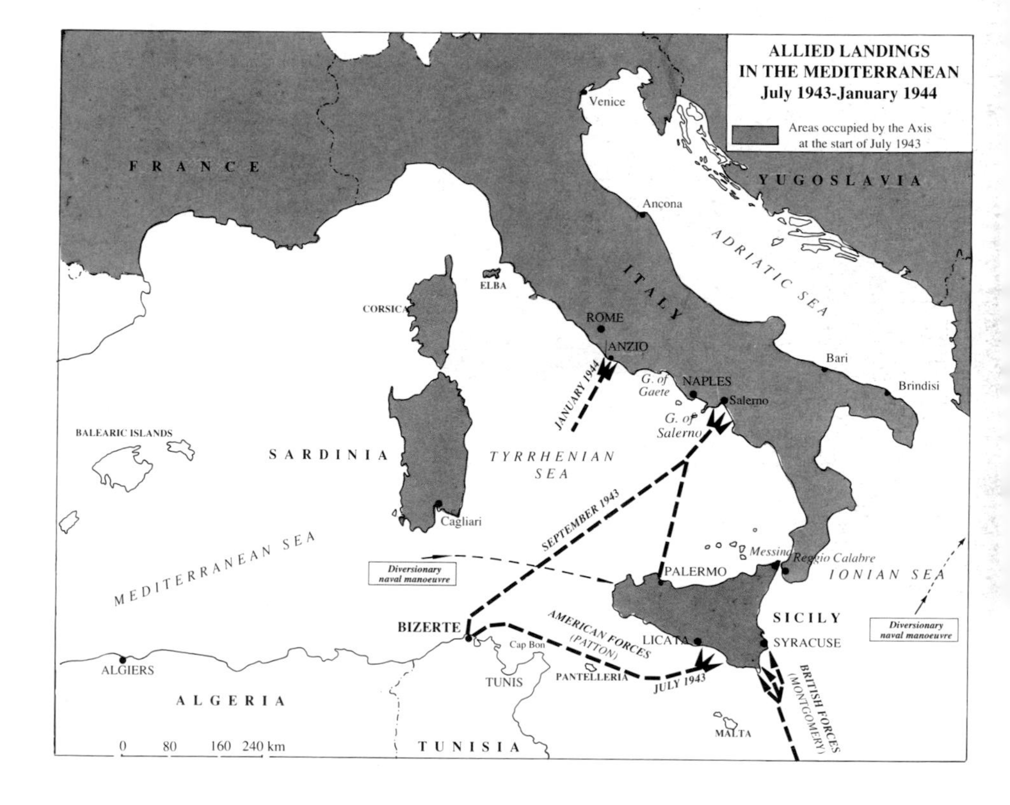

By mid-August 1943, after five weeks of violent combat involving almost half a million Allied soldiers, Mussolini was toppled and the island was freed. Using Sicily as a springboard, the Allies decided to push on into southern Italy: whilst the British and Canadians were to cross the Straits of Messina, on September 3rd, the US Vth Army of General Clark would land to the rear of the German defenders further north, in the Naples area, in the Gulf of Salerno.

SALERNO Avalanche

Executed against their wishes by the Americans, the landing at Salerno (Operation *Avalanche*) was on altogether a smaller scale than *Husky*. The same was true of the next operation, at Anzio, in January 1944. In a hurry to get the war over, after Sicily the American chiefs-of-staff had only one objective: to prepare the Allies' big return to the continent of Europe thanks to an assault to be launched from across the Channel in the spring of 1944. For General Marshall, chief-of-staff of the *US Army,* it was only from the bridgehead secured in the Bay of the Seine that the Allies could hope to see off the *Reich,* and not by dispersing their forces in several theatres of war. Faithful to this strategic approach, the Americans' part in the Italian operations was a half-hearted one.

In choosing to land at Salerno, the Allies' objective was to facilitate progress northwards up the peninsula for Montgomery's troops and capture the port of Naples which was crucial to get supplies to troops whose mission was to deliver Rome. From a strategic viewpoint, the possession of airfields in Italy would make it possible to bomb German cities from the south and also oilfields exploited by the Axis in Rumania.

Canadian troops landing.

Landing ship infantry with gangways.

Opposite, Canadian tank in Italy.

A dream setting

Launched in late summer 1943, Operation *Avalanche* took place in one of the most beautiful bays in the Mediterranean not far from Vesuvius, Pompei and the ruins of the Greek temple of Paestum. Cut off from the north by the Sorrente peninsula extended by the rock of Capri, the bay of Salerno, surrounded by an amphitheatre of hills planted with olive and pine trees, is a huge bight over 30 miles long. It was in this heavenly landscape that the Allies had decided to try their luck: the British would land in the northern sector, not far from Salerno, and the Americans in the south. Between the two assault sectors there was an intervening stretch about 7 miles long. The entire contingent was placed under the command of American general Mark Clark.

In spite of surveillance of the air space, the *Luftwaffe* spotted the 700 ships of the Allied armada responsible for escorting, and also supplying firepower and transport for the 55,000 men in the first assault wave (including the *Commandos* and the *Rangers*). Actually this discovery came as no surprise: after all, it was the day after the capitulation of Italy and in Berlin, they were expecting some sly move on the part of the Allies precisely in the Gulf of Salerno, which was perfectly suited to an amphibious operation and situated, moreover, in the vicinity of the port of Naples within striking distance of the fighters based in Sicily. The whole business got off to a bad start, especially since General Clark, commander-in-chief of the operation, had ruled out prior bombardment of the coastal defences in order not to give away the future assault sector to the enemy and also because the diversionary manoeuvre planned on Rome (parachute drop of General Ridgway's 82nd *US Airborne Division*) had had to be cancelled.

The *Panzers* again

Hardly had they left their landing craft than the attackers encountered serious resistance on all sides. On the evening of D Day, the junction of the two assault sectors had not been obtained, the planned objectives had not been achieved and the beachhead was lacking in depth. This was the moment, when the enemy was at his most vulnerable, that the Germans launched a violent counter-attack using mostly armoured vehicles. Under tremendous fire, the Allied troops had to fight fiercely against the *Panzers* in the midst of ruins dating back to Antiquity, oleander bushes and orchards of almond-trees. On September 11, when casualties were beginning to reach devastating proportions and the situation was near-catastrophic, Clark sent out a cry of alarm and was begin-

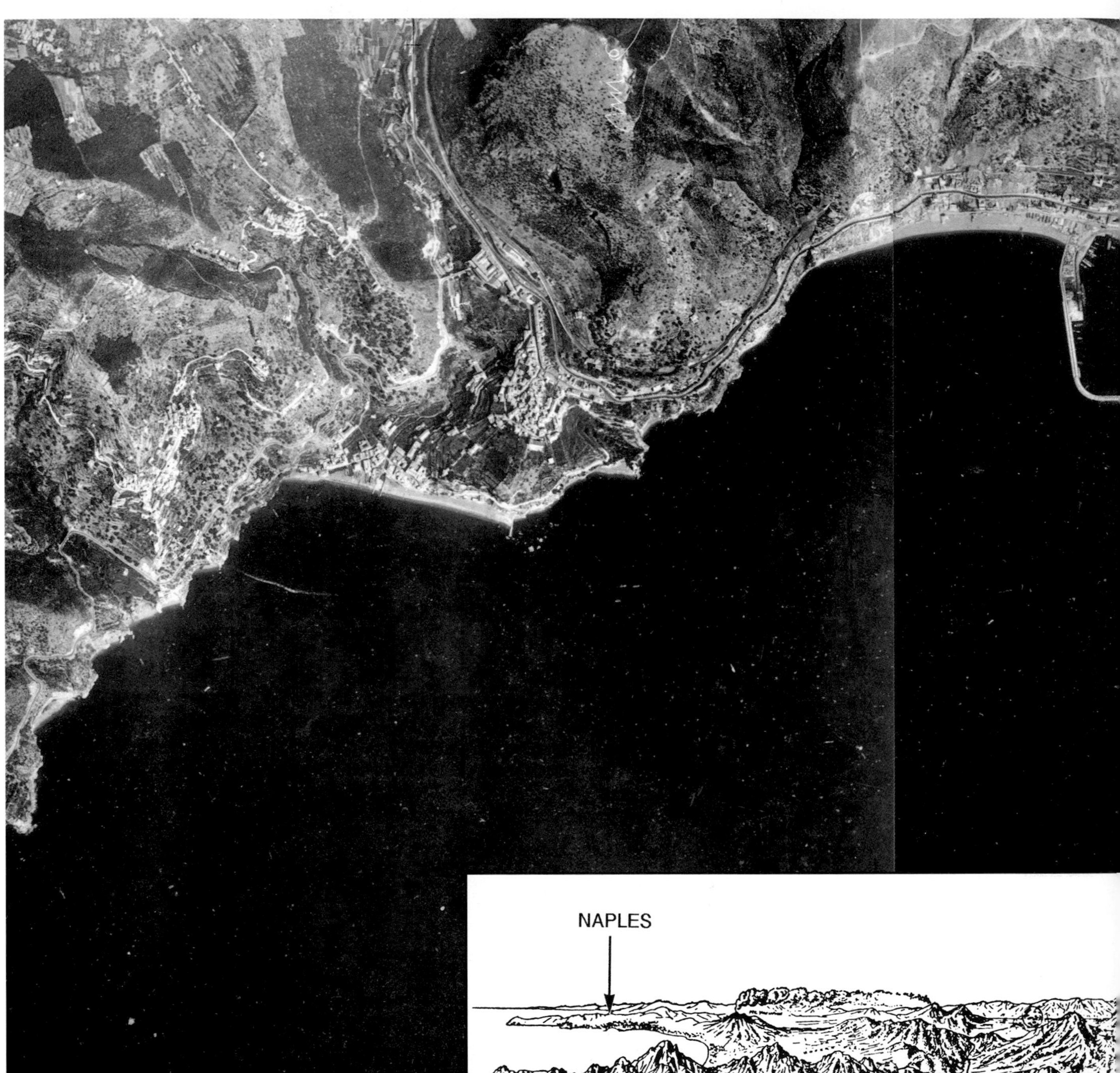

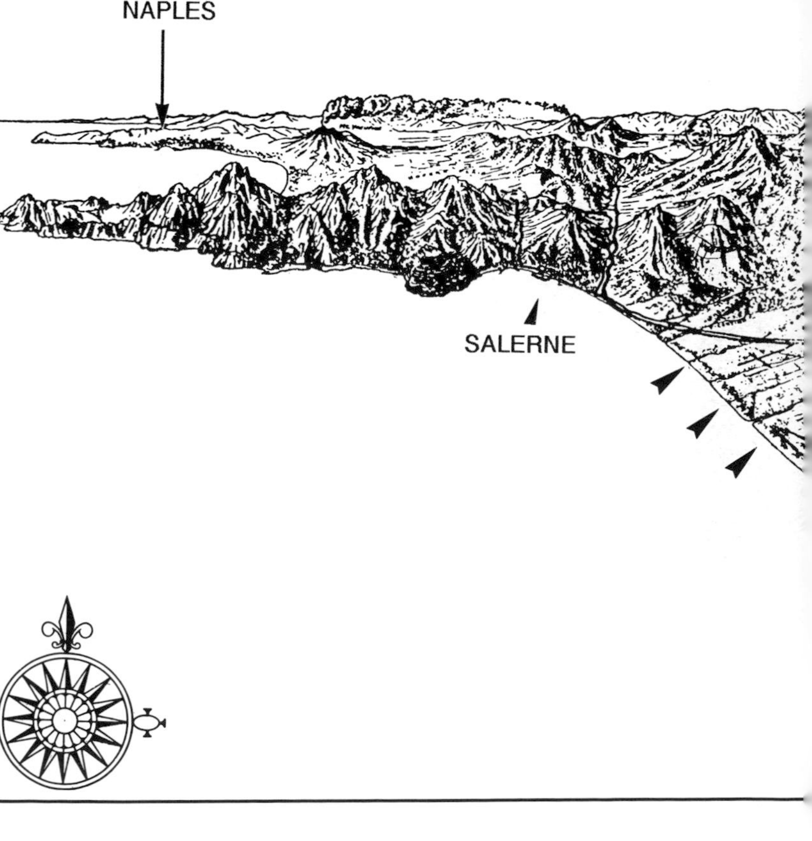

Aerial photograph of the northern end of the Gulf of Salerno. In the centre of the document the pier protecting Salerno harbour can be seen. The three-dimensional sketch was made from aerial photographs. The landings took place in the southern sector of the gulf, not visible on the photograph.

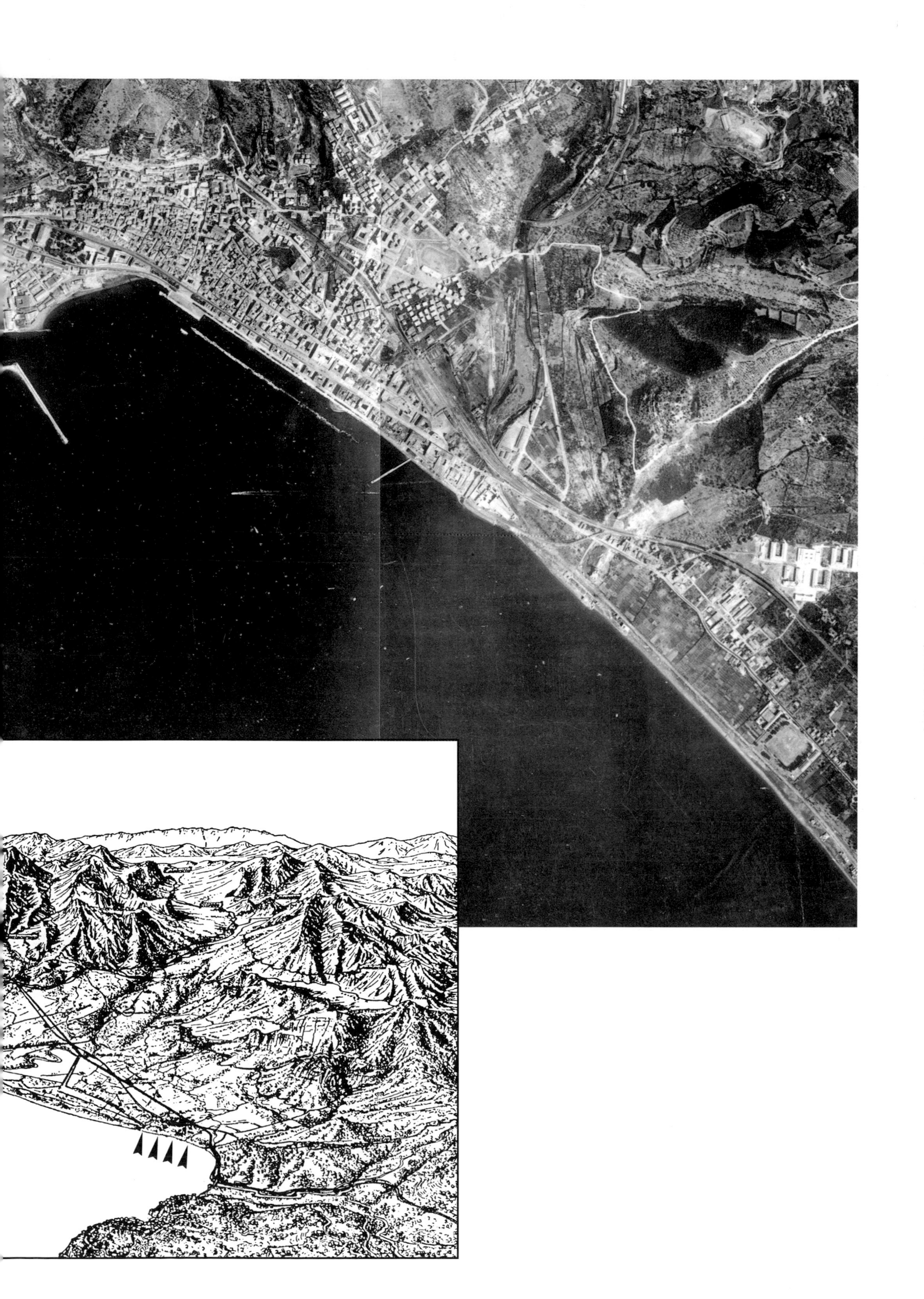

ning to think of evacuating the beachhead. In order to save Salerno, Eisenhower had to mobilize all his forces: he ordered the Navy to come in close to the shore and pound the German positions up to about twelve miles inland, and to land an extra tank division. All available resources in the Mediterranean theatre of operations were requisitioned and allocated to the transport of 82nd Division and matériel and engineers with the special task of constructing air-strips behind the beachhead. Thanks to this general burst of activity, by mid-September the situation had been saved; however, for a long time Clark still made little headway, sustaining considerable losses in the process. On October 1st, after three weeks of fierce fighting and 18 days behind schedule, the Allies came in sight of Naples, but they had no intention of dying. Three months later, at the end of 1943, Clark was still more than 75 miles from Rome. *It's a long way to Rome,* said German propaganda ironically! After coming so very close to disaster, the Salerno operation demonstrated the urgency, once a landing had been made, of losing no time in making quick progress penetrating inland, and gaining ground in order to put the beaches cluttered with matériel and the air-strips out of the range of enemy fire, whilst also attempting to link up the assault sectors. In short the manoeuvre was clear, a vigourous thrust was necessary to try to break out and create a single widened beachhead.

In order to release Clark's troops who had got themselves into a corner along the Tyrrhenian coast, and ease their progress up towards Rome, the commanders of the operation decided to launch a new assault against the rear of the German army, 35 miles further north, in the Anzio sector.

Italy. Canadian infantry.

Italy. Mules rendered great services to the Allies.

ANZIO
Shingle

As the objective of the Salerno landing had been to assist Montgomery's troops to break through northwards, the Anzio landing would enable the troops of General Clark blocked on the *Gustav* line to resume their march on the Eternal City. It had been hoped that, sandwiched between the two, the German 14th Army would give way. Comprising roughly 60,000 men placed under the command of the American General Lucas, the small Allied army landed at night on three beaches, on either side of Anzio and Nettuno, two small fishing ports approximately 35 miles south of Rome. The surprise effect was complete, and the landing was a success: in the first 24 hours, 35,000 men and more than 3,000 vehicles were brought ashore. More preoccupied with consolidating the beachhead he had secured than with making a thrust inland, General Lucas was to be surprised by the speed and violence of the German counter-attack under the command of General Kesselring. By engaging the *Luftwaffe* forces in huge numbers against the concentrations of ships and launching a simultaneous counter-attack on land with mostly armoured vehicles including miniature remote-controlled *Goliath* tanks crammed with explosives, the enemy pushed back the Allies, inflicting extremely heavy losses in the process. As at Salerno, three months earlier, there was a critical

Anzio. The Americans come ashore.

moment and once again, the intervention of the naval artillery and fighter-bombers was responsible for an almost miraculous recovery.
In the process, five thousand Allied soldiers had lost their lives and Anzio, like *Omaha* later on, remains in American and British memories as a symbol of perseverance and courage. For the strategists, on the other hand, Anzio is the example of a successful landing that was spoilt by the incapacity of the commanders to exploit their initial gains. The easily predictable outcome was that the Allied troops were pinned down for long months in the beachhead.
Although costly in terms of human lives, the Italian campaign immobilized 22 German divisions until the spring of 1944, compared with 8 on the eve of the landing at Salerno early in September 1943. If the 14 divisions that were thus neutralized in the Mediterranean peninsula had been on the western front, they could have spelled disaster for the Normandy landings. Just as the Allied operation in Sicily in July 1943 had relieved the pressure on the Soviet front and contributed to success at Kursk, likewise Salerno and Anzio played a part, if only an indirect one, in the Allied success in the Channel. This operation to come was certainly no foregone conclusion: the shores of the Bay of the Seine were after all defended by the famous Atlantic Wall!

Anzio. Reinforcements arriving for 5th US Army.

THE ATLANTIC WALL

"Hitler would invariably place the Atlantic Wall at the forefront of any assessment. Apparently indoctrinated by his own propaganda on the subject for so long and without having ever actually seen it for himself, he formed a mental picture of it based on the quantity of concrete that it had swallowed up, on the number of men working on it and on comparisons with the Maginot line fortifications. He based his judgement on photographs brought to him by his own photographers who were not military men, rather than on objective information supplied by the Wehrmacht authorities or their chiefs-of-staff."

General Warlimont

The ATLANTIKWALL

A linear defensive system on the model of the Maginot line, the day before the Allied operation in Normandy the Atlantic Wall comprised approximately 12,000 fortified works along the coasts of France. If we add to the concrete the thousands of guns and machine guns, the minefields on both land and sea, the hundreds of thousands of beach obstacles, the ditches and anti-tank walls as well as the flooded areas, we realize that the Wall was no mere bluff, as Marshal von Rundstedt would have had us believe, after the war.

Propaganda picture designed to intimidate and discourage the Allies.

The strength of the German defensive system was all the more surprising that the first systematic work to place defences along the coast of western Europe only started in the spring of 1942. Until this date, the biggest building sites opened by the German army on French territory were the five submarine bases at Lorient, Brest, Saint-Nazaire, la Pallice and Bordeaux and also various landing strips for the *Luftwaffe.* It was only towards the end of 1941, when the United States entered the war, that they started thinking in Berlin of putting up a defensive system along the coast. The American's entering the war increased the threat hanging over the rear of the German army at that time wholly committed to the merciless struggle on the Russian front. In order to prepare for the danger of a landing operation to the rear of the *Wehrmacht,* Hitler then took the decision to erect a line of fortifications on the shoreline of western Europe from Friesland to the Spanish border.

In August 1942, a few days before the Allied operation on Dieppe, he fixed the number of concrete works to be constructed at 15,000 and the number of men assigned to train the garrison of each bunker at 20. In a word, an army of 300,000 men would keep guard on the endless 2,500-mile stretch of coastline extending from northern Holland to Spain. German propaganda christened this defensive line *Atlantikwall* (Atlantic Wall). However,

"Er war ein ungeheurer bluff... (The Wall) was a gigantic bluff, not so much for the enemy, who knew very well through his agents and from other intelligence sources, as for the German people. Hitler never saw the Atlantic Wall nor even any part of it..."

Von Rundstedt

contrary to what the term wall might convey, it was in no way a continuous obstacle protecting the *Festung Europa* like ramparts surrounding a medieval castle. More like a fence or a string of pearls, the line of fortifications alternated strongholds with long sectors of lesser resistance. Bearing more resemblance by its dimensions to the Great Wall of China than the Siegfried line or the Maginot line, the Atlantic Wall was to be the biggest building works undertaken by the Todt Organization in France between the spring of 1942 and the spring of 1944. For its completion, this imposing programme had been divided up into several successive stages. The first and most important stage involved the fortification of those sectors judged to be most vulnerable (islands, large ports, subma-

"However, it is crucial that the enemy captures a port if he is to carry out a large-scale landing. This fact underlines the importance of the west coast ports. Accordingly, I have ordered that these ports be turned into strongholds."
A. Hitler

Brest. Submarine base.

rine bases, river mouths, low gradient beaches suitable for an amphibious operation...). As regards the density of the works to be built, the shore occupied by the 15th Army and extending from Le Havre to Antwerp was clearly a top priority. As we see, from the outset the German strategists had placed their bets on an Allied landing taking place north of the Seine rather than to the south and most probably in the immediate vicinity of a large port. The frontal assault carried out by the Canadians on Dieppe in August 1942 only made the German High Command even more convinced that the Allies were bound to need the installations of a large port in order for their operation to be successful. In blocking the main gateways to the continent when approaching from the sea by an accumulation of defensive means, the Germans were convinced that they had discovered the weak link in the Allied strategy.

A disconcerting operation

In actual fact, by choosing to land deep in the Bay of the Seine, on a relatively distant shore from the English coast and therefore less heavily fortified and what is more on open beaches between the ports, the Allies succeeded in throwing the defenders off balance. Further disorientated by the steady stream of false information broadcast by the enemy under Operation *Fortitude* and taken up in the reports of Colonel von Roenne, the German military, including Rommel, were led into thinking that the operation in Normandy was only a decoy and that they should expect the real invasion in the Pas-de-Calais. Even Hitler was taken in until the end of July by the campaign of deception led by Roenne, chief of the division responsible for assessing Allied military potential and for supplying intelligence regarding Anglo-American intentions. As a member of the conspiracy against the *Führer,* Roenne systematically exaggerated the number of American divisions stationed in Great Britain and about to cross the *Channel.* By pointing to the threat of a second Allied operation in this way, he encouraged Hitler in his refusal to reduce the strength of 15th Army. For his treachery and his part in the July 20 plot, Colonel Alexis von Roenne, one of those indirectly responsible for the failure of Rommel in Normandy, would be sentenced to death in October 1944.
A collection of decoys and all kinds of stratagems, *Fortitude* implemented on a vast scale all the usual methods of the secret services as well as numerous deceptions of its own, not to mention the key contributions of the French, Belgian and Dutch resistances. Thanks to the unexpected collusion of a few anglophilic German officers, the defenders were completely taken in by the Allied strategy of deception.

Atlantic Wall. Camouflaged observation post.

THE BUILDERS OF THE WALL

From March 1942, the defence of the coasts became a priority task.

Jobs available: JOINERS, CARPENTERS, LABOURERS. Good wage. Travel allowance. Company working for the occupying authorities. TECNOTRAMO, route de Paris, Champagne (Sarthe). V 1837, Le Mans.

It was the Todt Organization that was assigned the task of building the Atlantic Wall. Although little known to the general public, this, one of the more effective institutions under the 3rd Reich, was not on its first assignment of this kind.

The construction agency of the *Reich*

Between 1933 and 1938, the Organization created by engineer Fritz Todt had pulled off the tour de force of providing Germany with a network of autobahns, then proceeding from 1938 to build the 22,000 bunkers of the Siegfried line on the western border of Germany. The Todt Organization was thus accustomed to working with civil engineering companies, carrying out large-scale mobile building programmes to tight schedules, recruiting and providing board and lodging for hundreds of thousands of workmen.
After the start of the war, it was to the T.O., which had by then become the agency responsible for carrying out the Wehrmacht's construction projects, that the *Kriegsmarine* and the *Luftwaffe* would turn for the building of submarine bases and airfields. After the invasion of Russia, the T.O. was called to the Eastern front to repair roads and hydroelectric dams and adapt the railways to standard gauge. In the spring of 1942, after taking the decision to fortify the coastline of western Europe, Hitler appointed Speer, the new chief of the T.O., to oversee the execution of the work. To execute the vast programme of construction of the 15,000 bunkers with in the deadlines set by the *Führer* (the main superstructure to be completed by May 1st 1943), the technical chiefs-of-staff representing the Todt Organization were to mobilize about 200 German civil engineering companies. After contracting various work to the T.O., the German companies would in turn subcontract part of the work to French companies specializing in earth-removing work, concreting, road-building or digging underground works.

Standardisation

In order to gain time and give a certain defensive value to the line of coastal fortifications as early as possible, the engineers of the T.O. placed a certain number of standard blocks at the disposal of the armies allocated to the shore defences. Enabling the simplification of work order and estimates (volume of earth to be removed in digging foundations, supply of materials, labour requirements, construction deadlines...), standardisation presented the additional great advantage of making it possible to envisage mass prefabrication of certain elements (concrete beams, armour-plated doors, electrical and telephone equipment, ventilation ducts...). This excessive standardisation makes the Atlantic Wall a repetitive and monotonous fortification made up of thou-

Calais. German defences.

sands of grey concrete blocks more or less sunk into the ground. A far cry from the fortifications in the style of Vauban!

300,000 labourers

In order to procure *Arbeitskräfte* (labour), at the start of the war the Todt Organization called upon volunteers; later, non-compulsory enrolment being insufficient, the occupying forces contrived with the complicity of the Vichy authorities to create unemployment in the French economy by closing a certain number of companies declared to have no useful purpose for the war effort or to requisition foreign workers such as the Spanish Republicans who had sought refuge in France. These measures in turn proving inadequate, the Todt Organization intensified their propaganda campaigns based on high wages and the many bonuses available to volunteers taken on, also the guarantee that workers on the Atlantic Wall construction programme would not be deported to Germany. At the beginning of 1944, the Germans passed on their labour requirements directly to the French government. The Vichy authorities were given the task of spreading the load of German demands and fixing the contribution of each region. According to the archives, in June 1944, the Todt Organization had 300,000 men working on its building sites throughout France. Out of this total, roughly a third were Frenchmen and the other two thirds were foreigners, especially Soviet partisans, Poles and Czechs, all considered as doing hard labour. Treated like prison convicts, these men were condemned to mass producing bunkers.

Protected by a reinforced concrete canopy several metres thick, submarine bases, rocket installations and bunkers would bear witness for a long time to come to the presence and activity along the shores of France of a monster machine in the service of a demential will.

Many of the T.O.'s French foremen were former members of the L.V.F.

Two German engineers stationed at Caen wish to make the acquaintance of two ladies to go out together and improve their French. Send offers along with photograph to: Leuillot, 124 rue Saint-Jean, Caen, Calvados.

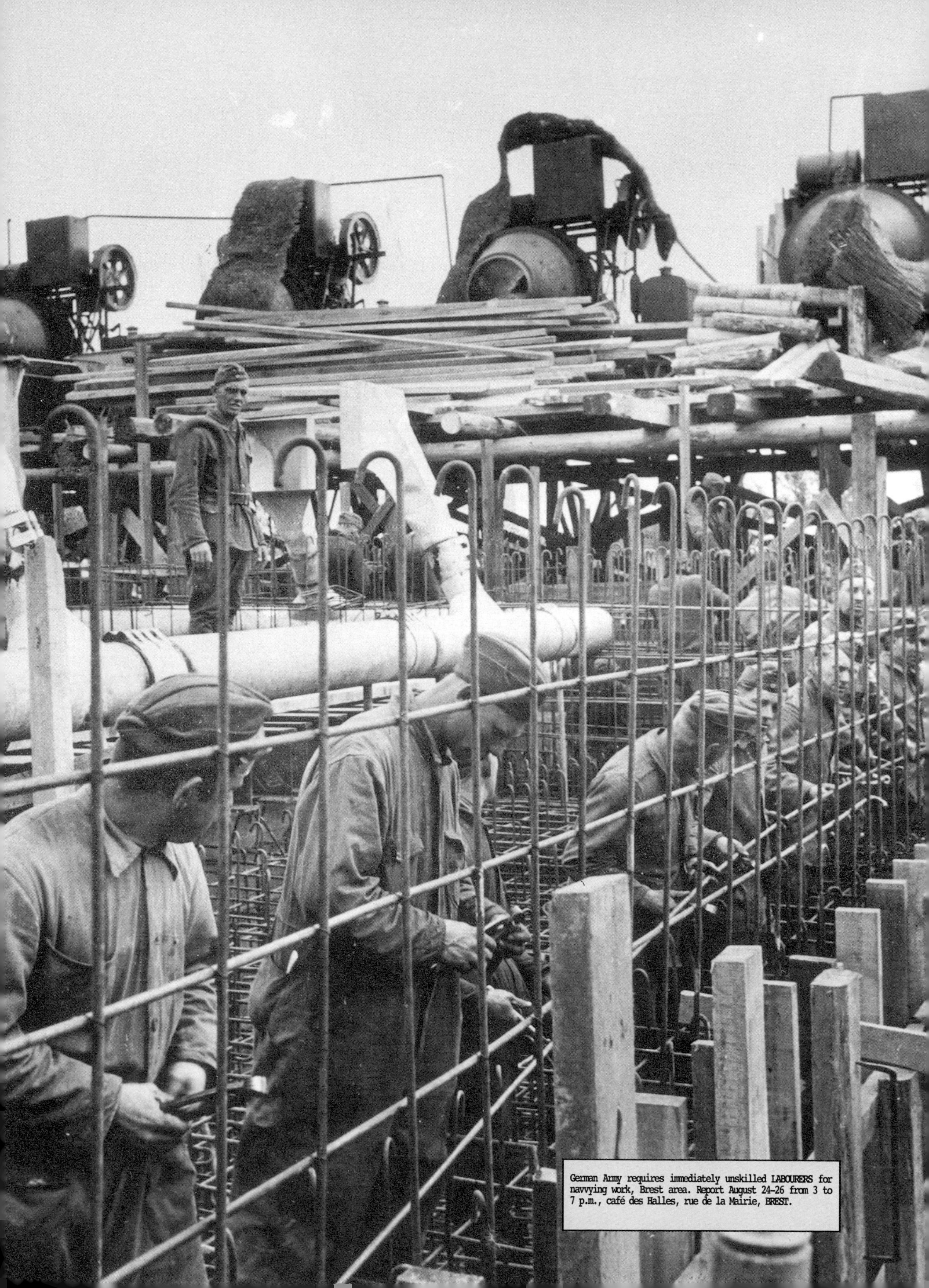

German Army requires immediately unskilled LABOURERS for navvying work, Brest area. Report August 24–26 from 3 to 7 p.m., café des Halles, rue de la Mairie, BREST.

THE GERMAN COASTAL BATTERIES

For lack of a navy or an airforce capable of providing seaward protection of the coasts of western Europe, the defence rested in June 1944 on a succession of artillery batteries scattered along the shoreline. We can estimate from German archives that at the moment of the Allied operation in Normandy, there were 800 gun positions on the shores of *Festung Europa* (Fortress Europe) with an approximate total of 3,000 guns. In accordance with Hitler's instructions, the biggest concentrations of defensive weaponry were to be found around the large ports (Dunkirk, Calais, Boulogne, Dieppe, Le Havre, Cherbourg...), on the edge of the gently sloping beaches of northern France and in the islands (Channel Islands, Cézembre, Groix, Belle-Ile, Ré...)

Platforms or casemates

The shore batteries were the most familiar elements of the Atlantic Wall and were the backbone of the coastal fortifications. These installations were allocated to the long-range defence of the shore, that is fending off an invasion fleet attempting to approach the coast. Housing various pieces of artillery, a battery generally comprised 4 guns and a few subsidiary installations. The guns allocated to covering the sea had originally been placed on circular concrete platforms surrounded by a low wall. With the increasing number of air raids, although the positions were cleverly camouflaged, the Germans were obliged to shelter the guns inside casemates. A casemate was a big cube-shaped bunker with a window opening out towards the sea, and comprised a gun room where the gun was housed and, to the rear, one or two small rooms used as munitions stores. Above the gun, several wide diameter vents sucked out poisonous fumes released into the gunroom after a few salvoes had been fired.

Lorient. Vestige of an armour-plated telemeter of a shore battery.

Command posts

Sited ahead of the gun positions, the command post was usually on two floors: an observation post for the lookouts with field glasses on tripods, a map-room and telephone exchange on the ground floor and, upstairs, the range-finding post protected by a concrete canopy as at Longues-sur-mer, near Arromanches, or open to the air as at the Pointe du Hoc. The link between the command post responsible for calculating firing coordinates and the artillery placed to the rear was obtained through underground telephone cables. Underground shelters used as barracks for the garrison or ammunition stores were scattered around in the vicinity of the blockhouses. Defended by tank or machine gun turrets, by searchlights, ditches, minefields and barbed wire, each artillery posi-

La Dilanne. Observation post on three levels.

“Wer alles defendieren will, defendiert gar nichts...”

“He who would defend everything, defends nothing...”

Frederick the Great

tion was an entrenched camp along the shore.

Guns from all over Europe

In order to equip its numerous coastal batteries, the *Reich* had salvaged pieces of artillery from all the arsenals of Europe. In this way, in the Bay of the Seine, between the Pointe de Barfleur and the Cap d'Antifer, there were around forty batteries totalling a little over 150 guns along a seventy mile stretch of coastline. Among these, there were pieces of Russian origin at Ver-sur-Mer, Czech 210-mm calibre guns at Saint-Marcouf (behind *Utah Beach*) or at Merville (4 100-mm guns) and especially French guns taken from army stores, from the Maginot line or French coastal forts (old 194, 164, 155, 138, 120 or 95-mm guns...). Polish or Austrian guns were to be seen elsewhere along the coast. In a word, weapons from a good half-dozen countries and of more than a dozen different calibres were used to defend the Wall. This wide variety of tubes made maintenance, spare parts supply, instructions for use and ammunition supplies a major headache and ruled out the construction of standardised gun positions.

Cézembre. Shore battery on a platform.

Fort Vert. Calais. Swivelling casemate resting on the roof of a bunker.

THE GERMAN RADAR STATIONS

Arromanches. Würzburg Radar sited on the upper cliff. Opposite page: British radar on the southern coast of England.

It was vital for the defenders not be caught by a surprise invasion. Hence the Germans had intelligence services in various neutral countries who from time to time sent reports and information regarding the Allied build-up, and also a line of radar stations along the coast of western Europe. Working on the principle that electro-magnetic waves are reflected when they come against an obstacle, these radar devices were available to give the alarm. The detection stations were fitted out by the *Kriegsmarine* or the *Luftwaffe* and installed at regular intervals.

Freya and *Würzburg*

The main long-range detection centres combined several types of appliance working on several different wave lengths at a time for technical reasons and also to avoid Allied jamming. By associating several different devices, it was hoped that the detection centres would not all be disrupted together and that it would always be possible to use intelligence supplied by the radar that was the least affected. Two types of device were used along the shores of Europe, the *Freya* and the *Würzburg*. With a range of up to 65 miles, the *Freya* with its characteristic rectangular antenna was used for long-range exploration. Alongside this super sentry, the *Wehrmacht* also had the *Würzburg,* an appliance with a distinctive parabolic antenna. Designed by the Telefunken firm, the *Würzburg* operated at decimetrical wavelengths which allowed for great precision in detection (target altitude, distance, composition). Together these two electronic eyes, the one specialising in long-range detection, the other in close-range detection, gave the *Wehrmacht* a definite edge at the outset of war.

A revolutionary radar device

The lead gained by German technology in the field of detection was to be short-lived. The Allies had set their physicists to work on exploring a new direction, that of very high frequencies or ultra short waves which had infinite possibilities for detection. The Germans discovered this lead gained by the Allies in early 1943, when they shot down in Holland a British bomber equipped with a radar that had demanded more than a year of research to perfect by the teams of Allied scientists. Using ultra short waves, this revolutionary device, codenamed H2S, gave the navigator a panoramic screen on-board, which displayed a picture of the ground being flown over! The German military could not believe their eyes!
For the *Reich,* valuable time had been lost and the *Wehrmacht* would have to be content with improving the performance of the two basic appliances already available. From the *Freya,* an extremely cumbersome radar named *Mammut* was devised which specialised in the exploration

"Our knowledge of the German defensive set-up became more and more thorough during the course of 1942, thanks to the rapid development of a network of agents specialized in the search for intelligence on the subject of radar, and to neutral friends who brought us intelligence on the occupied countries. Speaking of "agents" and of "neutral friends", it is only right to make special mention of the Belgians. In 1942, they provided roughly 80% of all the intelligence we obtained in this field, including a map of the greatest importance stolen from the command of the searchlights and radars of the northernmost of the two sectors organized in Belgium for the German night fighters."

W. Churchill

of naval space and a gigantic radar known as *Wassermann.* With a range of over 190 miles, it could detect from Cherbourg bombers taking off from airfields sited in the very heart of England! As for the *Würzburg-Riese,* a hundred of which had been placed along the shores of France, it could raise the alarm to the fighters about ten minutes before the arrival of an enemy air formation, flying at speeds of around 340 mph. In all, it may be estimated that between Dunkirk and the Hague peninsula, there were more than a hundred radar sets capable of detecting an approaching invasion fleet.

Jamming

If the benefits of surprise effect were to be maintained, a major factor in the success of any military undertaking, the most dangerous stations of the Bay of the Seine had to be knocked out either by advance bombing raids or by an electronic jamming operation. This interference designed to blind the screens at the German detection stations would be carried out by a naval and air fleet during the night of June 5 to 6. If we are to believe the post-war written account by Admiral Krancke, commander of the German naval forces on the western front, in spite of the general breakdown of the detection system, one radar station sited in the Val de Saire, east of Cherbourg, did make out at around 3.00 a.m. that something unusual was going on in the western half of the Bay of the Seine and more precisely off Port-en-Bessin, without however being able to gauge the size of the target. Although com-

Auderville-Hague. An American photograph showing the grid of a German radar guarding the coast in its concrete well.

ing on top of the numerous messages indicating that gliders and paratroops had landed in various parts of lower Normandy since midnight, according to Krancke this warning was taken seriously neither by Marshal von Rundstedt, commander-in-chief in the western theatre of operations, nor by General Speidel deputising for the absent Rommel as commander of Army Group B. After all, back in November 1943, hadn't Hitler dispossessed von Rundstedt of part of his command by relieving him of the preparation and conduct of the struggle against the Anglo-American invasion, appointing Rommel to this job? As for the flegmatic Speidel, one of the officers who had joined the anti-Hitler resistance circle, during this decisive night he was to come round to the opinion of von Roenne who claimed that the Germans should stay where they were. He was encouraged in this wait-and-see attitude by the analysis of the previous amphibious operations carried out in Sicily and the Italian peninsula. During these last three landings, had not the Allies landed their troops in complete darkness? At three or four o'clock in the morning, nowhere had any landing on the Normandy beaches been reported. Keeping calm, Speidel refused to consider the situation to be serious even after the discovery by a German patrol, in the wreckage of a British glider, of a map that gave a fairly good idea of the scale of the Allied operation. Rommel's deputy would start wondering from 6.30 a.m., the time the seaborne landings began at *Utah*. Precious hours had been lost, and more vital hours were to be wasted waiting till the *Führer* woke up.

Operation aimed at jamming German radar by dropping tinfoil in the sky.

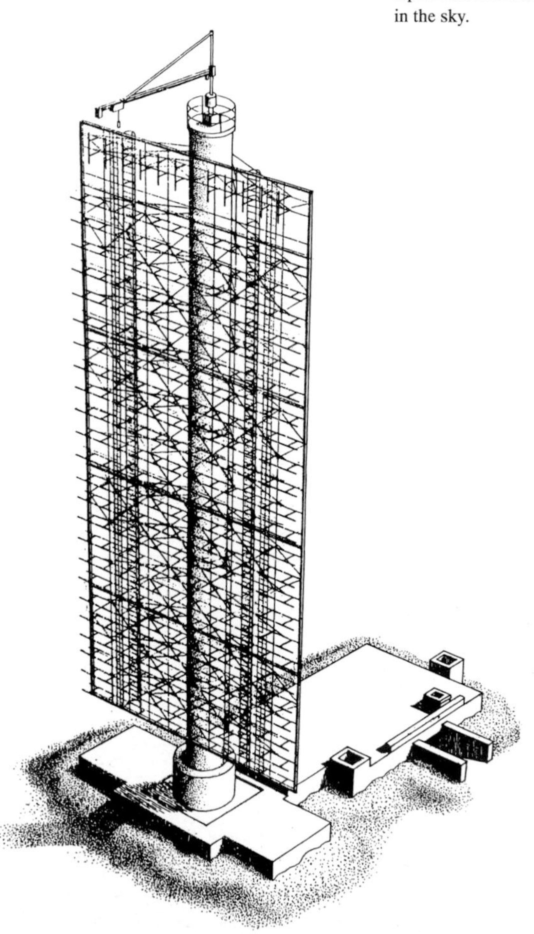

Wasserman radar.

THE SMALL WORKS

Consisting of *Regelbauten,* i.e. standardised blocks, the beach works made up a widely varied set. The diversity of this category of bunker can be explained by the fact that the many and varied requirements of the armies responsible for defending the shore (observation, transmission, detection, energy production, storage, repairs, shelters, firing...) all had to be satisfied. Unlike the large shore batteries whose function was to prevent an enemy fleet from approaching the coast, the beach works had the task of providing close-range defence of the shore. To these blocks fitted with one or two gun slits and a small calibre gun or machine gun, or concrete niches with an old tank turret on top, was assigned the mission of fighting off landing craft, armoured vehicles trying to advance towards the beach exits or assailants having set foot on land.

The category of passive defence works had an even more varied range of blocks. We may include in this family the command posts often topped by an armoured bell with a panoramic sight or equipped with a periscope emerging through the protective concrete casing, telephone exchanges, radio stations, shelters for electricity generators (engine-room, storage tanks, transformer...), for searchlights, guns, tanks, stores, workshops, munitions bunkers, garages... We may add to this list the shelters that served as troop barracks (kitchen, mess, dormitory, infirmary...).

The last type of passive defence works comprised underground passages. In these vaulted and concreted tunnels the same technological solutions were used in the struggle against water infiltration, air replenishment and energy supplies.

Guarding a cove.

Rommel inspecting the beach defences.

THE WEHRMACHT IN THE WEST IN 1944

Marshal Hugo Sperrle.

Like the Maginot line, the Atlantic Wall was an inert system. Designed to impede the attackers or slow down their progress inland, the concrete rampart alone was incapable of giving victory. This could only come from the intervention of the armed forces stationed in the vicinity of the fortified complex. The outcome of the Allied amphibious operation depended not on concrete but on the power, the scale and speed of the German counter-offensive. What then was the fighting potential of the *Wehrmacht,* the day before the invasion?

A reduced navy

Comprising roughly 100,000 men, the German naval forces on the western front were placed under the authority of Admiral Krancke. Apart from the submarines, the German naval forces in June 1944 were incapable of opposing any serious resistance to the Allied navies. On the coasts of the North Sea, the Channel and the Atlantic Ocean the *Kriegsmarine* had a few dozen ocean-going ships (destroyers, torpedo boats, patrol boats...) plus a handful of small units (merchant ships or fishing vessels converted into mine-sweepers...) responsible for protecting coastal waters. To these forces were added a few dozen submarines based in the West under Admiral Dönitz. At the time of the invasion, the action of the German naval forces would be fairly slight. Faced with the impressive array of resources deployed by the Allies, the submarine attacks were hesitant and uncertain. The torpedo-launches from Le Havre on the other hand turned out to be more aggressive.

A decimated air-force

With a wealth of human resources, the 350,000-strong German air-force on the Western front was placed under the authority of Marshal Sperrle commanding the 3rd *Luftflotte.* Just like the navy, in June 1944, the *Luftwaffe* was incredibly weak. Decimated by the British and American fighters, evicted from airfields close to the coast, with a little under 1,000 aircraft the 3rd *Luftflotte* was unable to maintain air supremacy over France. However, after reinforcements arrived from the *Reich,* aircraft marked with the swastika did cause the Allies a few headaches after June 6 with their mine-laying activities each night in the Bay of the Seine.

An incoherent command structure

With no navy or airforce capable of bringing effective opposition to bear on the Allies, the defence of the shore rested almost exclusively on the shoulders of the land army. Although a million men were present behind the fortification besides another 450,000 marines and airmen, the army placed under the command of Marshal von Rundstedt was seriously flawed. Worn out by three years of war on the Russian front, the divisions suffered a cruel lack of means of transport (gun carriages, trucks), were partly

A German plane in an awkward position.

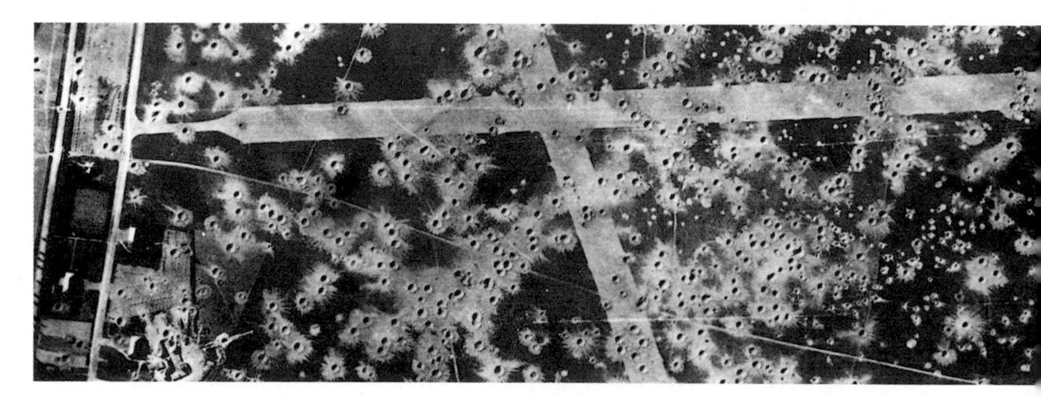

How an airfield looked after an Allied bombing raid.

composed of foreign units *(Osttruppen)* of doubtful patriotism and were equipped with an odd mixture of outdated weapons. According to General Zimmermann, von Rundstedt's chief-of-staff operations officer and the author of an interesting report on the war in the West, material shortcomings were not the most serious problem. This high-ranking German officer reserved his most biting criticism for the defective command structure, namely the excessive centralisation of power in the hands of Hitler, the total absence of any coordination between the three services, and the dividing of authority.

Von Rundstedt and Rommel, at Saint-Germain-en-Laye.

Rivalry between von Rundstedt and Rommel

The dispute between von Rundstedt and Rommel on the question of the stationing and use of the mobile reserve comprising about ten armoured divisions was definitely a contributing factor towards the success of the Allied undertaking. This was the striking force of about 1,500 tanks that had been assigned the task of throwing the Allies back into the sea. Having failed to come to any agreement as to how to use the *Panzers,* the assault force ended up being split between the two commanders. This fractioning was to have disastrous consequences at the time of the invasion. Instead of a powerful offensive, the Allies had to face nothing worse than a series of isolated piecemeal attacks that they had no trouble in countering. With no clear strategy, the anti-invasion struggle was an undertaking that was doomed to failure. To this day, the philosophies of Rommel and of Rundstedt are the subject of lively debate. Who was right? That is a difficult question to answer. However, the experiences of Gela, in Sicily, of Salerno and Anzio show in all three instances the failure of the counter-attacks launched by the *Panzers* due to overwhelming Allied superiority in the air and the intervention of naval batteries. Given that, whether the tanks were on the coast or far to the rear would probably have made no difference to the final outcome of the battle, with the possible exception of *Omaha...*

High morale

Far removed from all these rivalities between their commanders, the troops maintained staunch discipline and remained confident. In certain units, as in the 12th SS *Panzer Division Hitlerjugend* where morale was particularly high, the grenadiers could not wait to get the opportunity of measuring up to the Allies. In the Carentan sector, the American paratroopers of the 82nd and 101st Divisions would encounter fierce resistance from the young volunteer paratroops of Colonel-Baron von der Heydte's 6th *Fallschirmjägerregiment.* Two months later, when the military situation had worsened and seemed hopeless for the German 7th Army, half surrounded in the region of Falaise, General Schimpf commanding 3rd Paratroop Division did not hesitate to proclaim in a declaration broadcast to his troops that the Allied unit capable of capturing 3rd Division was not yet born! Indeed as it turned out, Schimpf walked away from all the ambushes that were set for him, and was to fight it out to the bitter end!

Very different from such boasting was the atmosphere at supreme command level and Army Group B command level where Rommel responded to Rundstedt's resigned indifference with pessimism and discouragement. In short, according to Zimm Rommelermann, the German Western command had been overcome by the vague feeling that the situation was hopeless and that the combat to come was an unequal one.

Panther Tank, in Normandy.

D DAY

"Soldiers, Sailors and Airmen of the Allied Expeditionary Force! You are about to embark upon the Great Crusade, toward which we have striven these many months. The eyes of the world are upon you. The hopes and prayers of liberty-loving people everywhere march with you. In company with our brave Allies and brothers-in-arms on other Fronts, you will bring about the destruction of the German war machine, the elimination of Nazi tyranny over the oppressed peoples of Europe, and security for ourselves in a free world... I have full confidence in your courage, devotion to duty and skill in battle. We will accept nothing less than full Victory! Good luck! And let us all beseech the blessing of Almighty God upon this great and noble undertaking".

General Eisenhower's Order of the Day for June 6 1944

THE OVERLORD PLAN

Above: German soldier surveying the Channel.
Opposite page: fitting a camera inside an aircraft.

It was at the Quebec conference, in August 1943, that General Morgan, the Chief-of-Staff called upon to draw up plans for the big return of the Allied armies to the continent of Europe, exposed the broad lines of his project. Codenamed *Overlord,* the operation, designed to push back the Axis forces and liberate the continent of the German occupation, envisaged a powerful attack in the Bay of the Seine, on the Normandy coast. Initially, the Allied assault was to be carried out early in May 1944 and take place between the Orne and the Vire, on a front nearly thirty miles long, and three divisions were to be engaged.
At the beginning of 1944, the initial plan was partially reworked at Montgomery's request. The main modification involved widening the assault sector, considered to be too narrow. Thus, the invasion front first envisaged was extended to the west with *Utah Beach,* and to the east with *Sword Beach.* Out of the new total of five beaches, three were given to the British and the Canadians and the two others to the Americans. Taken in its widest sense, the assault sector extended from Sainte-Marie-du-Mont to the Orne estuary, a distance of approximately 50 miles.
The extension of the invasion front in turn demanded that increased numbers be engaged (three airborne divisions instead of two brigades and five infantry divisions instead of three). If we include the paratroops, the infantry and the sappers, it now became necessary to get 156,000 men ashore on D Day. Right up till the last minute, this increase in forces allocated to the initial thrust obliged Eisenhower, the Supreme Commander of Operation *Overlord,* to postpone the Normandy invasion until June 1st 1944 in order to have another month in which to gather together the extra requirements in gliders and especially assault craft.

Why Normandy?

The first task that had to be resolved by *COSSAC* (name of the Allied chief-of-staff responsible, from the spring of 1943, for drawing up the main outlines of the plan of the cross-Channel invasion operation) was to select an assault sector from the long stretch of shoreline extending from Denmark to the Spanish border. In order to make his choice, *COSSAC* took into account various elements such as the distance from the British airfields, the presence of a big port in the neighbourhood of the assault sector, the existence of low gradient beaches, a hinterland likely to be suitable for the building of airstrips and for tank movement, and lastly, the strength of the Atlantic Wall shore defences. Combining these different factors, *COSSAC* came up

AERIAL PHOTOGRAPHY

Longues, June 6 1944.

with a short-list of two coasts, the Pas-de-Calais and the Bay of the Seine. Of the two sectors, the Pas-de-Calais unquestionably presented the greater advantages (nearness to Britain allowing maximum air support and a quick turn-around time for the ships, the presence of numerous ports, the shortest route to the heart of the *Reich*...), but the strength of the German coastal defences was such that the assault was in real danger of being transformed into a bloody disaster. On the other hand, although much further from the airfields and ports of Britain, the coasts of lower Normandy had a considerable advantage in that they could be cut off from the rest of France by destroying the bridges across the Seine and the Loire. Apart from this strategic edge, the shores of lower Normandy were only lightly fortified, with long beaches protected from the prevailing winds by the Cotentin peninsula and had two deep channel ports in Cherbourg on one flank and Le Havre on the other.

After much debating, *COSSAC* expressed the opinion that the shore extending between the Orne and Vire estuaries was more suited to a large scale amphibious attack and would make a useful starting point for subsequent operations. In short, at the beginning of July 1943, a few privileged military leaders knew the date (May 1st 1944) and the place (the Bay of the Seine) of the big operation that was to take the Allies back into western Europe.

Aerial photography

During the Second World War, aerial photography, which had already been used during the First World War, became very important as the main source of information about the enemy for the High Command. For these aerial photography missions, in order to escape the enemy fighters the Anglo-Americans used specialized squadrons of high speed planes capable of reaching relatively high altitudes, including *Spitfires,* and later on twin-engined *Mosquitoes* or American *Lightning* fighters minus their heavy armament. With the increased speeds of the aircraft (300 to 375 mph), it became necessary to improve the performance of the cameras fitted under the fuselage or in the nose of the plane by improving the lenses, the quality of the films and especially the speed of the moving pictures. This is how cameras with no shutter and continuously winding film came into their own.

Depending on requirements, two types of photographs were produced. The commoner type, the overhead photograph, was taken from an altitude of roughly 30,000 feet, which, given the standard focal length used, meant that photographs were to a scale of

Longues-sur-Mer. On the aerial photograph on the left taken by the RAF on March 2 1944, some work is visible north of the village (road construction across the fields, excavations, bunkers built along the clifftop...). On the right hand photo, dated May 22, the extent of the building work is evident: four casemates, magazines, shelters, paths, zigzagging trenches, combat positions... Using aerial photographs, the commanders could follow the progress of work on the German defensive system.

Above: Dieppe. Air attack against the radar station *(Freya* and *Würzburg)*.
Opposite page: production of strips of tinfoil for the jamming of German radar.

approximately 1/10,000. These pictures were extremely clear and were later used to produce topographical maps of the future invasion zone. The Allies had at the time for France nothing but some old out-of-date mapping documents, in particular the ordnance survey 1/80,000 black-and-white sheet maps. Of doubtful accuracy, and on too small a scale, such documents, which had not been updated since their publication, were hardly adequate for the Normandy operation. In addition to overhead photographs, the commanders also required oblique angle pictures of the coastline. Taken from just above sea-level, roughly 3/4 mile off the Normandy coasts, such pictures provided an excellent view of the coast as seen from out at sea. When placed side by side, these large-scale (1/2000) photographs gave a panoramic view of the coastline, enabling pilots on board the D Day assault barges to find their way with ease and come ashore on the right beach.

Thanks to high and low altitude aerial photography, whether overhead or oblique, the Allies had almost perfect knowledge of the coastline of the lower Seine and the hinterland, prior to the invasion. They knew the position of the enemy's large shore batteries, radar stations, antitank ditches, V.1 rocket launching sites... Similarly, they had gained many vital pieces of information about the future field of battle: the breadth of the rivers, location of flooded areas, density and rate of flow of the communications channels, the whereabouts of impracticable sectors for armoured vehicles and heavy materials, sectors suitable for setting up campaign airstrips, munitions dumps or fuel stores... Once the landing had taken place, aerial photographs would enable observers to monitor the progress of operations on land, spot the enemy's movements, obtain advance warning of enemy manoeuvres and assess his weaknesses or the extent of damage caused by the air bombardment.

In spite of the fact that this method supplied the command with more than three quarters of all intelligence obtained from the enemy, aerial photography also had some notable lapses. In Normandy, for instance, the aerial photography interpretation services failed to give sufficient warning of the fact that the large 155 mm guns in the Pointe du Hoc emplacement had been replaced with telegraph poles covered with camouflage netting. As it happened, German artillerymen had moved the pieces of artillery on gun carriages one night the previous April, nobody in the sector had had knowledge of the move and hence this valuable piece of information had not been

"It had been found that strips of paper with one side metallised, such as is often used to wrap up chocolate, were quite sufficient, if cut to the right length, to reflect radio waves strongly. Bundles of strips of this sort, weighing only a few pounds, thrown out of an aeroplane would flutter down in clouds several yards across and give Radar echoes almost exactly like those produced by ordinary bombers... Our bombers came to hear of it and wanted to use it at once to save their machines. But the snag was obvious. The device was so simple and so effective that the enemy might copy it and use it against us... Fighter Command accordingly wanted the secret kept at any rate till we had found an antidote."

W. Churchill

passed on to London. One can imagine the disappointment of the *Rangers* on discovering the deception early in the morning of June 6. It was the same story in the British sector with the battery at Merville. Going, this time, on the size of the casemates, the RAF's aerial photography interpreters had come to the conclusion that the bunkers at Merville housed large-calibre guns. With such firepower, they were capable of turning the operation of bringing the assault troops ashore on *Sword Beach,* on the morning of June 6, into a veritable bloodbath, so the guns had to be disabled by a special action conducted by paratroop commandos of *6th Airborne Division.* In actual fact, after capturing the gun emplacement at great cost, the paratroops discovered that the bunkers housed nothing more than low-range guns made in Czechoslovakia and incapable of reaching the sector of the Brèche d'Hermanville. Intelligence networks had of course studied the battery and obtained details about the emplacement, the anti-tank ditch and the position of the machine-gun nests, but no information as to the calibre of the guns that had been installed in the firing chambers, until after the departure of the French workers requisitioned by the Todt Organization. In its war diary, the *Suffolk Regiment* detailed to capture the German strongpoint codenamed *Hillman* and situated in the town of Colleville (now Colleville-Montgomery), just behind the beach, spares no criticism with regard to the aerial photograph interpretation service. Everything, from the size of the position, the extent of the mine fields, the complex network of trenches, to the fire power and size of the garrison, had been under-estimated, hence the unpleasant surprise awaiting British combat troops on the morning of D Day, and the delay in their march on Caen.

Similarly, the American paratroopers of 82nd Airborne were in for an unpleasant surprise, during the night of June 5 to 6, on discovering the extent to which the valley of the Merderet had been flooded. These deadly marshes had not been picked up on the aerial photos doubtless because of the tall grasses had grew in the water, creating an illusion of firm ground. Apart from aerial photographs, the other big sources of information for the Allies were the interrogation of captured prisoners and, of course, information supplied by the resistance networks.

Any landing operation involves air superiority for the attacker.

The Trappes sorting station, after a bombing raid.

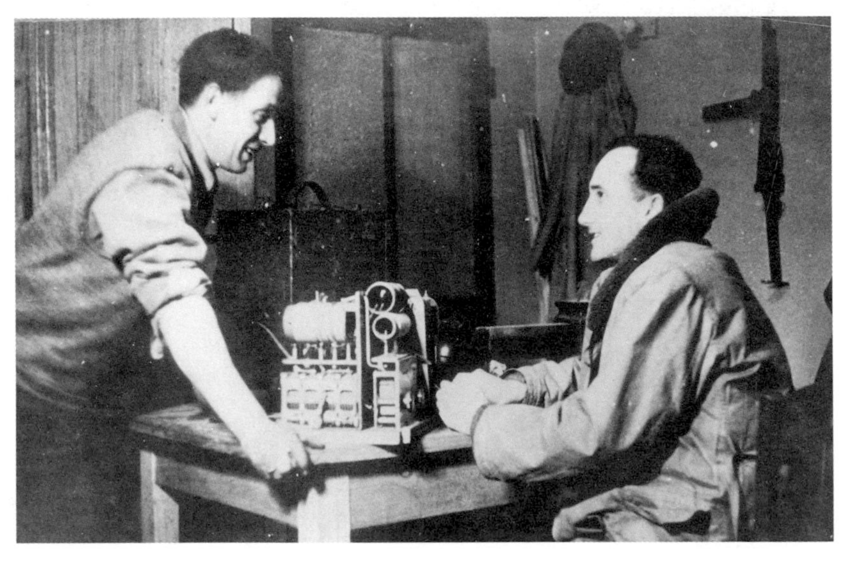

Underground fighters transmitting intelligence to London.

FINAL PREPARATIONS

Bombing of a bridge across the Seine at Mantes.

Whilst British and American shipyards had become an incredible hive of activity, building assault craft and sections of the artificial harbours, in early spring of 1944, the Allied air force began a vast bombing campaign against the road and rail communications networks in north-western France. This campaign was aimed at destroying bridges and tunnels, railways and sorting stations, etc, in order to paralyse the traffic and delay the arrival of German reinforcements on D Day to the future beachhead. At the same time, the big bridges across the Seine and the Loire were bombed in order to isolate Brittany and Normandy from the rest of France.

In April, a bombing campaign was begun against the coastal defences of the Atlantic Wall (shore batteries, radar stations, rocket bases and launching sites, munitions dumps...). Between April 10 and June 5, 2,500 Allied aircraft took part in attacks against the coastal installations situated in the future assault zone. In order to avoid revealing the chosen objective, 6,300 sorties were also aimed at targets outside the invasion sector. From April 10 to June 5, Allied aircraft carried out a total of nearly 9,000 flights and dropped 23,000 tons of explosives on the coastal fortifications along the Atlantic Wall.

During these final months, in Britain, the land forces detailed to lead the assault organised numerous invasion exercises, landing personnel, tanks, vehicles and equipment. These rehearsals were carried out by day as well as by night, and both provided them with valuable experience and brought about various improvements. By the spring, each man knew what it was to attack a beach in a landing craft with bullets flying in all directions and shells exploding at close quarters. The paratroops of British 6th Airborne Division, for their part, had reconstituted in close country in England an exact replica of the Merville battery, one of their objectives during the night of June 5 to 6, on the basis of indications supplied by air photographs. Similarly, as soon as he was briefed as to his objective, to capture the battery at the Pointe du Hoc, Colonel Rudder, commanding the 2nd *Ranger* battalion, was off training on cliffs of the Isle of Wight similar to those in the Bessin. Meanwhile, intensive observation work off the Normandy coasts was being carried out by teams of officers of the *Royal Navy* shipped across in specially adapted LCP craft. When they arrived within sight of the coast, on moonless nights, the frogmen climbed into inflatable dinghies and went ashore. They then had to collect samples of the sand, just a few yards from the Atlantic Wall fortifications, to check

Above, on June 6, the Allies used over a thousand gliders.
Following page: a practice drop for 6th *Airborne Division.*

FORTITUDE

for the presence of shallows and determine the nature of the sea bed, where the large *Phoenix* caissons for the artificial harbours were to be sunk. Never had an amphibious operation been prepared so methodically and precisely, nor concealed with such intelligence and cunning.

An elaborate deception plan

In order to draw the attention of the defenders of the beaches away from the Bay of the Seine, a plan of deception had been laid by the Allied secret services for the German high command. Grouped under the code-name *"Fortitude",* the diversionary activities devised by London were twofold: *Fortitude* North was designed to mislead the enemy into believing that the Allies were building up for an invasion of Norway, and *Fortitude* South that the invasion sector was to be the Pas-de-Calais.

So as to increase fears that the landing would take place in Norway, in the region of Trondheim, the Anglo-Americans concentrated ships in the north-eastern ports of Britain, began mine-laying operations in the waters of the North Sea and the Baltic and set off a series of attacks against the submarines off the coasts of Norway. As regards the Pas-de-Calais sector, where the Germans were expecting the invasion to take place, the Allies piled up various sections of the artificial harbours in the ports along the eastern coast of England facing Boulogne, carried out numerous bombing raids against shore batteries between Dieppe and Dunkirk as well as laying mines at both ends of the Straits of Dover and placing the French and Belgian resistance movements on the alert. Further inland, again with the intention of reinforcing the German high commanders in their convictions, they turned out whole squadrons of dummy military equipment including inflatable rubber lorries, tanks and jeeps and also dummy airfields for wooden planes. At the same time, intense wireless traffic

Preparing for D Day.

Horsa gliders.

Aircraft arriving in Britain from the United States.

Admiral B. Ramsay.

was simulated between the fictitious command posts throughout the region. All these measures were designed to contribute to fostering a climate of uncertainty and misleading the enemy. In May 1944, in one of the last of his weekly reports, von Rundstedt, commander-in-chief in France, clearly stated that the sector under the greatest threat was unquestionably the coastal area to the north of the Seine. What is much worse, events would subsequently show that as late as the end of July 1944, both Hitler and Rommel were still convinced that *Overlord* was no more than a diversionary operation and that the real invasion would take place in the Pas-de-Calais. Hence the *Führer's* adamant refusal to weaken his defences along the front north of the Seine in order to strengthen the troops in Normandy.
Intended to blind the enemy, Operation *Fortitude* continued throughout the night of June 5 to 6, with the dropping of dummy paratroopers in the region of Yvetot (near Rouen), Maltot, south-west of Caen, and Marigny, near Saint-Lô. During this famous night, again with the intention of deluding the German command, the Allies simulated the approach of a vast invasion fleet on the screens of the radar devices installed by the enemy between the Cap d'Antifer and Fécamp (Operation *Taxable*), in the Boulogne region (Operation *Glimmer*) and off Barfleur. At the same time, a fleet of 262 ships packed with electronic jamming equipment was detailed to neutralise German remote detection devices positioned in the Bay of the Seine.

At high tide or at low tide, by day or by night?

If a moonlit night was the obvious choice for the launching of the biggest military operation of all the time, insofar as the aircraft and glider pilots would be able to find their objectives, on the beaches, both night and day assaults had their supporters. At the top, this controversy was the subject of fierce argument between General Montgomery, commander of the land forces, who favoured an initial attack under cover of dark and at high tide, and Admiral Ramsay, who advocated a daylight assault. After much discussion, it was finally decided to mount a dawn assault, quite simply because the risks of collision due to manoeuvring errors amongst the hundreds of craft pressed up against each other along the beaches would be too great in the dark. As for the choice of tide, it was the visibility of the obstacles planted on the beaches, between the low and high tide marks, that would settle the question. In order that the landing craft

Beach obstacles, on the Brittany coast.

Do's and don'ts

DO remember that the enemy must have information and will stop at nothing to get it.
DO grasp that intelligence is built up by piecing together small items of information, like a jigsaw puzzle. You may consider that the scrap of information which you can give away is of no importance but it may supply the missing piece and reveal the whole plan.
DO understand that a breach of security instructions may cost your life, and the lives of thousands of your comrades, and the success of a
MAJOR MILITARY OPERATION.
DON'T give away:- your port of embarkation,
the name of your ship...
the date or time of sailing
your destination or route...
DON'T pass secret information to ANYONE - not even your family and lifelong friends. How can you expect them to keep it dark, when YOU have let it out to them?
DON'T be provoked by anyone's stupidity to show that you know better. He may not be as stupid as he looks.
DON'T drink if you can't hold drink and your tongue too.
DON'T try to send messages in code. The enemy are better at reading codes than your pal or the girl you left behind you.
FINALLY.
DON'T think that, because you hear someone giving away secrets, it won't matter if you do the same. Two blacks do not make a white.

Leaflet issued
to the Allied soldiers

Above: The Allied commanders at Southwick House.
Opposite page: Douglas C.47s in formation, the plane used for paratroop transport and for towing the gliders.

4th June. *We met at 4 a.m. at Southwick House. Some of the convoys had already sailed, working to a D Day of the 5th June. The weather reports were discouraging. The Navy reckoned the landing was possible but would be difficult... I was for going. Tedder, Deputy Supreme Commander, was for postponement. Weighing all the factors, Eisenhower decided to postpone D Day for 24 hours; it would now be on the 6th June.*

5th June. *We met at 4 a.m. A heavy storm was blowing in the Channel... But the Met. reports indicated a slackening of the storm and a period of reasonable weather on the 6th June... On that, Eisenhower decided to go. We were all glad.*

B.L. Montgomery "Memoirs"

Allied fighter pilot ready for take-off.

should not be ripped open by the lethal mines on top of inclined stakes, the landings would have to take place at low tide or on a gently rising tide. This double constraint restricted the dates available for D Day: there are not many days a month when the tide is low just a few minutes before daybreak. Given the tidal conditions in the Bay of the Seine, it was arranged for the assaults to be staggered in time starting with Utah Beach and ending with Sword (last to land).

As to the day that would see the start of the biggest Inter-Allied undertaking in history, it was originally set for June 5, which left the 6th open as an alternative to fall back on, and the 7th another possibility. After postponing the operation for 24 hours due to bad weather, Eisenhower took the historic decision on Sunday June 4, around 9.15 p.m., in the library of Southwick House in Portsmouth, which for several months had been used for Admiral Ramsay's headquarters. A few hours later, the thousands of ships making up the liberation armada, the biggest fleet that any Admiral ever had under his command, set off towards the coasts of lower Normandy.

In spite of plenty of amphibious experiences in the Mediterranean or in the Pacific, no operation in any theatre of war had come any where near the complexity of the Normandy landings. In Africa, Torch had been mounted against undefended and not entirely hostile shores. In Sicily and in southern Italy, the Allies had landed on non-tidal shores that were little fortified and encountered only tok en resistance from the Italian units. Anzio had taught nothing new, except to confirm the supporting role that the naval firepower could provide for the newly-landed troops. In the Pacific, the landings mostly took place on isolated islands in a hostile jungle. Although valuable lessons had been drawn from all these experiences, the invasion in Bay of the Seine remained largely an unknown quantity: was it not against shores where the tides were of great amplitude, in a region with extremely changeable weather conditions, with beaches obstructed by murderous obstacles and closed off by walls or anti-tank ditches and swept by rapid fire from guns hidden in small pillboxes? As Eisenhower would later stress, the outcome was by no means a foregone conclusion. This is why in order to break through this section of the Atlantic Wall, over a total length of fifty miles, the Allies had gathered together a formidable striking force including 7,000 vessels, 11,000 aircraft, 160,000 men and 20,000 vehicles. Under such an onslaught, from the early hours of June 6, the most gigantic fortification, according to German propaganda, of all time collapsed.

A view of part of the Allied armada.

Casemate in the Atlantic Wall.

June 5. *"2145 hours, message from the wireless interception service concerning reception at 2115 hours of messages over London radio whose meaning is known and announces invasion is imminent. Consequently, all chiefs-of-staff concerned have been informed by telephone and alerted by 2nd Bureau, with the extra information that acts of sabotage planned in the event of invasion, and even in some circumstances insurrectional movements, may be set off".*

von Rundstedt
"O.B. West War Diary"

JUNE 6 1944 OPERATION OVERLORD

Chronologically, the June 6 operation can be divided into three stages: the airborne landings, the aerial and naval bombardments, and the seaborne landings with craft running up onto the shore.

The airborne landings

The assaults launched from the air marked the start of the large-scale operation. Performed at either end of the invasion zone, the objectives of the parachute drops were to protect the seaborne offensive along its flanks. In the eastern sector (in the region of Ranville), the 6th Airborne Division under General Gale landed by parachute. Apart from the mission to protect the beachhead against any counter-attacks launched by the German 15th Army, the 6th Division was to capture the battery at Merville, the bridges on the shipping canal from Caen to the sea and on the Orne, and destroy various crossing places on the Dives in order to hinder any counter-attack. On the opposite flank, in the Cotentin (in the region of Sainte-Mère-Eglise), the parachute landings were carried out by 82nd and 101th Airborne Divisions. Here again, these elite American troops were to capture certain fortifications or roads that had not been flooded and also destroy certain bridges. Due to wind, cloud, the violence of the German flak, sudden evasive action taken by the pilots and the flooded areas themselves, these airborne operations resulted in devastating losses.

General Gale.

Below: towing the *Horsa* gliders.
Opposite page: Paratroopers from 6th Airborne Division.

June 6. *"Between 0525 and 0555 hours, a continuous stream of messages reporting parachute landings and the approach of enemy ships throughout the region between the Orne and Saint-Vaast, whilst the wireless reports a large number of enemy units and warships in the western Channel..."*

June 6. *"0715 hours, message from 7th Army reporting that the centre of gravity of the enemy landings is between the mouths of the Orne and the Vire, and the centre of gravity of the enemy parachute drops behind those rivers, also in the area north of Carentan".*

von Rundstedt
"O.B. West War Diary".

Pegasus Bridge. Opposite: Major Howard's three gliders.

The aerial and naval bombardment

The pounding of the artillery positions by the RAF and the US Air Force had begun at the start of April. In the two months preceding the assault, the air force had carried out a total of nearly 9,000 sorties and dropped 23,000 tons of bombs on the German defensive system. During the night of June 5 to 6, 2,500 bombers would drop nearly 8,000 tons of explosives on the ten largest batteries in the future assault zone. This was the most violent air attack mounted by the RAF to date. Due to a dense layer of cloud, the bombings produced very uneven results, particularly in what was to be the Omaha sector. In addition to the disruption caused to the artillery positions by the creation of numerous craters (to this day clearly visible at the top of Mont Canisy or the Pointe du Hoc) and the destruction of underground communications cables, the terrific explosions had a definite effect on the morale of the garrisons shut up inside the concrete blockhouses.

At dawn, taking over from the air force, the naval artillery entered the fray. With this intention, a bombing fleet consisting of cruisers, battleships, torpedo boats and destroyers had taken up position facing the shore, on the morning of June 6. The bigger ships were placed on either flank of the sector opposite the more powerful batteries at La Pernelle and Saint-Marcouf to the west, Houlgate, Canisy and Le Havre to the east. The firing began at daybreak, half an hour before the troops were due to land. At that moment, it was light enough for observers in spotter planes circling above the German positions to direct and correct the aim of the warships' large guns. The results of the naval bombardment were spectacular although they were unable to silence the shore guns once and for all. However unbelievable it may seem, the coastal batteries failed to hit a single large Allied unit taking part in the naval bombardment! On D Day, the landing craft had more trouble with underwater mines, beach obstacles and manoeuvring errors than with the poundings of the shore batteries. There was at any rate an overwhelming disproportion between the hundreds of thousands of tons of concrete that had been poured along the seafront to protect the Atlantic Wall artillery emplacements and results obtained in the final showdown.

Above and opposite page: Air cover for the assault fleet.

Observing a bomb attack against the shore.

Radar surveillance on board an Allied bomber.

"Der seit langem erwartete Angriff der Britten und Northamerikanen gegen die northfranzösische Küste hat in der letzten Nacht begonnen."
Die Wehrmachtberichte.

"The long-awaited British and American attack against the northern coast of France commenced last night."
Communiqué of the *Wehrmacht* on Berlin radio

Above: Passing from the transport ships into the landing craft.
Opposite page: Canadian propaganda poster.

The seaborne landings

Due to variations in the times of the tide, the seaborne landings were to be staggered, starting in the west at *Utah* and moving gradually eastwards to *Sword.*
The mission entrusted to the US 4th Infantry Division (General Barton) was to establish a beachhead on the eastern seaboard of the Cotentin *(Utah Beach),* link up with the airborne units and with those who had landed at *Omaha.* Their next objective was to cut off the Cotentin peninsula from the rest of France, capture the port of Cherbourg and break out towards the South. On *Utah,* the assault was going according to plan and by the evening of D Day, a firm lodgement had been secured and there were few casualties. However, although enemy resistance had been relatively weak, at midnight the division had not achieved all its objectives.
The task entrusted to the US 1st Infantry Division (General Huebner) was to establish a beachhead codenamed *Omaha* between the Vire and Port-en-Bessin, then to head off south in the direction of Saint-Lô whilst at the same time deploying so as to link up with the neighbouring beach forces of *Utah* and *Gold.* The assault on *Omaha* was to encounter many difficulties and came very close to total disaster. It was only in late morning that the Americans got a firm and definitive foothold on the beach, with the arrival of extra reinforcements and a final surge of bravery. In the afternoon, when German resistance began to weaken for lack of adequate reserves, the attackers managed to break through the line of coastal defences and capture the village of Vierville. Meanwhile, the sappers cleared the beach of obstacles, filled in the ditches and cleared exits towards the hinterland. At the cost of appalling losses, the Americans had finally won the day.
To make a success of the assault on *Gold Beach* was the task of the 50th British Division (General Graham). Its mission was to create a vast perimeter with a view to putting the future artificial harbour at Arromanches out of range of the German artillery, and afterwards to link up with the Canadians from *Juno.* In spite of fierce resistance from the fortified emplacements at Le Hamel and La Rivière blocking the advance of the division, the attackers managed to occupy the hills over the future mulberry at Arromanches as well as the heights above Port-en-Bessin. In this port, in the very heart of the assault area, the Allied command had decided to set up an oil terminal which was to supply the entire expeditionary force. By evening on June 6, having established a firm foothold on the continent, the 50th Infantry Division had succeeded in joining up with the Canadians of *Juno Beach.*

1944

1944

YEAR OF DECISION

"The supreme effort has still to be made".

Rt. Hon. W. L. Mackenzie King

UTAH

A Marauder of the 9th Air Force flying over the US invasion fleet off *Utah.*
Below: American soldiers of 82nd Regiment at the foot of an anti-tank wall.

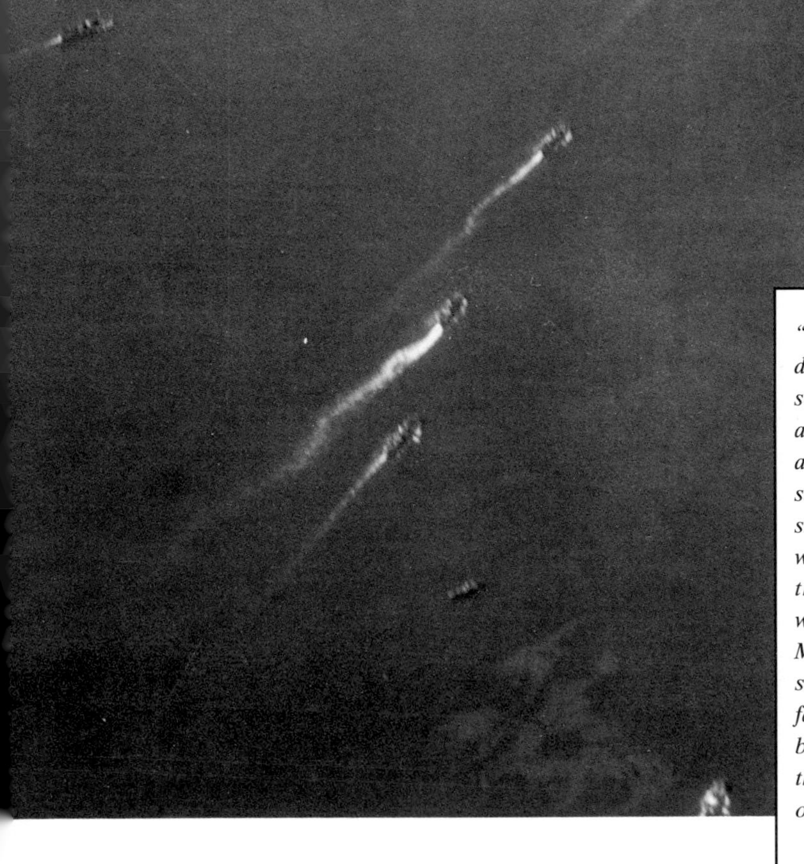

"On the seaward face of the dunes there was a concrete seawall about four feet high, and there in the dry sand above the tidemark, among such familiar seaside things as shells and sea-weed and cork washed up from fishing nets, the leading two companies were pausing; and there Mabry learned why he had not seen any of his landmarks. So far the battalion's landing had been easy; but it had landed in the wrong place... they were over a mile too far south."

David Howarth
"Dawn of D Day"

OMAHA

"Under the command of General Eisenhower, Allied naval forces, supported by strong air forces, began landing Allied armies this morning on the northern coast of France."
Official Communiqué n°1, from Supreme Headquarters, Allied Expeditionary Forces.

Views of Omaha on June 6 1944.

US

GOLD JUNO

The 3rd Canadian Infantry Division (General Keller) were given the task of disabling the coastal defences in the Courseulles-Bernières sector, then to break out into the interior in the direction of highway 13 and Carpiquet airfield, whilst also deploying to form a continuous bridgehead with the British from *Gold Beach* to the west, and *Sword* to the east. In spite of severe losses in landing craft caused by mined obstacles covered by the tide, the 3rd Division captured Courseulles and headed off towards the interior. They soon encountered German defences determined to sell their skins dearly in the sector of Tailleville and the radar camp at Douvres-la-Délivrande. Although they managed to link up with the British from Gold Beach at Creully, the 3rd Canadian Division failed either to wrest highway 13 or Carpiquet from the enemy. The front line positions reached on the evening of D Day would remain practically unchanged for over a month.

It was the 3rd British Division (General Rennie) that had been allocated the task of capturing the town of Caen, on the evening of D Day, at the same time linking up with the 6th Airborne Division that had been dropped on the east bank of the Orne, and with the 3rd Canadian Division that had landed to its right. After the liberation of Ouistreham, carried out with the help of the Franco-British Kieffer commando, the division encountered stout resistance before the high ground at Périers-sur-le-Dan *(Hillman)*. The time lost in reducing this nest of fortifications was sufficient for the Germans to take up a solid defensive position to the north of Caen and enabled them to block the advance of the British towards the capital of lower Normandy for more than a month.

Ver-sur-Mer, June 6 1944.

General Keller commanding the 3rd Canadian Infantry Division at Bernières on June 6 1944.

"At three thirty, this morning, the government was officially informed that the invasion of western Europe had commenced... Let all Canadian hearts be lifted up today in a silent prayer for the success of our forces and those of our Allies and for the liberation of Europe, as soon as possible".

Mackenzie King, Canadian Prime Minister.

The Canadians come ashore.

SWORD

The 3rd British Division lands at Hermanville.

Soldiers of the 45th Royal Marines Commando, on the morning of June

"Suddenly, through a gap in the smoke, the underwater defences, stakes and "hedge-hogs" entangled with barbed wire, loomed up before us. We had arrived. With a bump, our barges had just run aground. At this precise moment, the land and the sea seemed to be lifted up with a thunderous noise: mortar bombs, shells whistling overhead, the annoying barking of machine-guns, everything seemed to be concentrated on us. In a flash, the ramps were lowered. The first group, wearing green berets, made a dash for the beach, but a few seconds before the second group followed them, a 75 mm shell ripped the ramp off the barge in a heap of torn wood and metal... The big question was: "Were we in front of our landing point?" Yes we were. The demolished walls of the children's holiday camp where we were supposed to muster for the assault, once we had got across the beach, was straight in front of us..."

Commandant Kieffer

THE DEFENDERS COUNTER-ATTACK

The overall response of the occupying forces to the Allied assault was fierce but the strength of this resistance would vary from service to service.

Without ever endangering the Allied operation, the forces of the Kriegsmarine in the Channel turned out to be extremely aggressive. Although they only had a smattering of small units, half of which were based at Le Havre, where the occupying forces had built a large concrete shelter, the German navy was in action every night against the concentrations of ships of the Allied fleet. With the help of torpedoes, the Schnell-Boote (high speed patrol boats) managed to sink several units and create confusion among the landing fleet. In order to put a stop to the comings and goings of these patrol boats, the air force proceeded to bomb the naval base at Le Havre on June 14. This air raid, which destroyed or damaged around fifty ships, and another to follow over Boulogne, sounded the death knell for the activities of the Kriegsmarine in the Channel.

Since the beginning of 1944, the 3rd Luftflotte (3rd air fleet) had been incapable of commanding the air space in the west, and when the invasion came, it was to put up a much poorer showing than had been anticipated. According to Allied reports on D Day, less than a hundred German fighters flew over the assault sector, ten to twenty times fewer than what Allied military experts had forecast! The first appearance of a swastika over the beaches was not until Tuesday June 6, at around 3 p.m., i.e. about 9 hours after the start of the seaborne assault and 15 hours after the first paratroops had landed!

As it turned out, the fiercest resistance came on land, from the shore-based divisions (709th, 352th and 716th), the 91st Division of the Luftwaffe, the 6th Paratroop Regiment, and lastly from the tank units (21st Division, Panzerlehr and 12th SS Armoured). The latter unit had undergone intensive training and was raring to take up the challenge. They had been waiting for the big showdown with the Allies for weeks, and were determined to prove their superiority and give the Anglo-Americans a hiding. Up against soldiers like this, who had no intention of giving an inch of ground, preferring to fight without mercy to the last man, the Allies would pay a high price for final victory.

German anti-aircraft machine gun.

Rommel, right, Speidel, left.

The Germans Discover the American Plans

Too good to be true, this could be the title of the story that follows. In the evening of June 6, some soldiers of the 439th Battalion of the Eastern troops that had been incorporated into the German 352nd Infantry Division discovered in the mouth of the Vire, in the wreck of an LCA that had come aground on the ebb tide, the body of an American officer who had been killed at the time of the Utah landings. Miraculously the American officer still held fastened to his wrist a brief-case containing various documents. Among these papers, according to a report by 352nd Division's intelligence officer, there was a plan of operations for 7th US Arrmy Corps, a formation whose brief was to cut the Cotentin in two and capture Cherbourg! It was an extraordinary find. Forty-eight hours after the start of the cross-Channel invasion, the defenders had under their very eyes the plans indicating the Americans' scheduled movements in Normandy! The heavens had just given Rommel what the agents of the Abwehr had not been able to give him! From 352nd Division's intelligence officer, the documents were passed on up the normal channels till they reached Saint-Lô and the headquarters of 84th Army Corps under General Marcks, then to Le Mans and the offices of 7th Army. At this point Pemsel, Dollmann's chief of staff, made a detailed analysis of the documents and passed on a summary that reached Rommel's headquarters at La Roche-Guyon early in the morning of June 8, and on again to the headquarters at Saint-Germain-en-Laye of Marshal von Rundstedt, supreme commander on the Western front. From there, the news reached the Chancellery in Berlin. According to General Pemsel, the scale of the operations envisaged by the Americans in their documents (the capture of Cherbourg, then the invasion of Brittany) required so many troops that these operations automatically ruled out any second landing in the north of France. In spite of this clear-sighted analysis, Hitler continued to hold the opposite view. Full of mistrust, the German dictator could not help considering his troops' discovery as a ploy and a stratagem of the Allied secret service. Nothing could change this deep conviction: in Hitler's opinion, there were still several dozen Allied divisions in England waiting to cross the Pas-de-Calais. A second landing was imminent and this time he would not be taken by surprise.

The cemetery at Ranville.

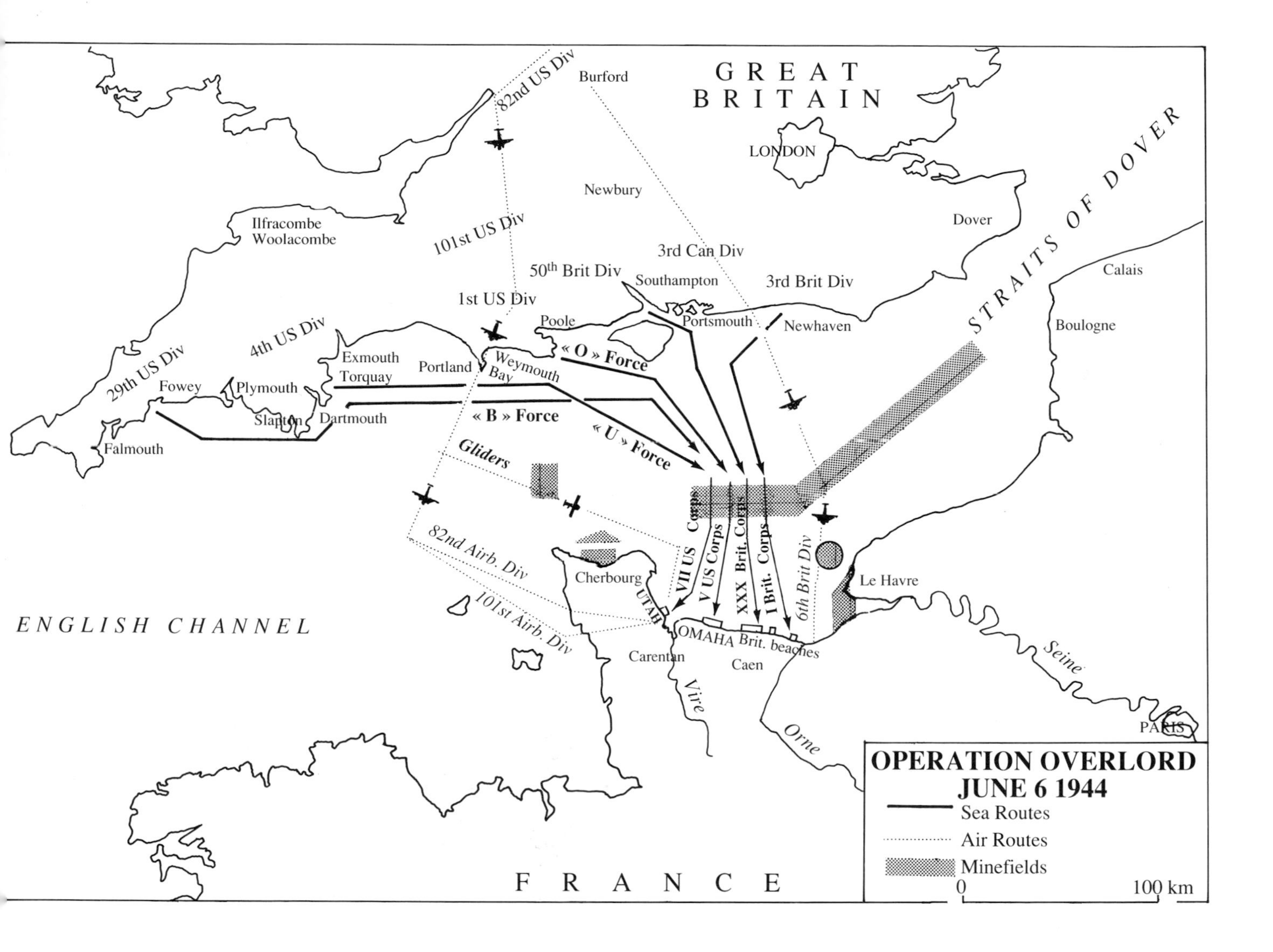
GREAT BRITAIN
LONDON
Burford
Newbury
Dover
STRAITS OF DOVER
Calais
Boulogne
Ilfracombe
Woolacombe
82nd US Div
101st US Div
50th Brit Div
1st US Div
3rd Can Div
3rd Brit Div
Southampton
Portsmouth
Newhaven
Poole
4th US Div
29th US Div
Exmouth
Torquay
Portland
Weymouth Bay
« O » Force
Fowey
Plymouth
Slapton
Dartmouth
« B » Force
« U » Force
Falmouth
Gliders
82nd Airb. Div
101st Airb. Div
Cherbourg
UTAH
VII US Corps
V US Corps
XXX Brit. Corps
I Brit. Corps
6th Brit Div
Le Havre
OMAHA
Brit. beaches
Carentan
Caen
Vire
Orne
Seine
PARIS
ENGLISH CHANNEL
FRANCE
OPERATION OVERLORD
JUNE 6 1944
Sea Routes
Air Routes
Minefields
0
100 km

THE SITUATION ON THE EVENING OF D DAY

On the evening of D Day, the Allies had managed to obtain a foothold on the continent. More than 150,000 soldiers had been landed by air and sea, together with approximately 20,000 vehicles of all types. On the whole, Overlord was a success and Eisenhower could be satisfied with what had been accomplished on the ground with a great deal of courage and suffering by gallant men. Certainly, the objectives set for the evening of June 6 were not all attained, but there was no question of complaining or throwing in the towel. This was not the spring of 1940! Now that the beachhead had been secured, it had to be consolidated prior to breaking out.

To paraphrase the speech made by Churchill at Mansion House in London on November 10 1942, the day after the British victory at El Alamein in Egypt, the Allied leaders could observe on the evening of June 6 that the Normandy invasion maybe did not put an end to the war but at least the success of this operation meant that, from now on, the end of the beginning was well behind them and the beginning of the end could not be too far off!

Without a shadow of doubt, one of the most momentous achievements in 20th century world history had just taken place in Normandy.

A British newspaper announces the Allied landings in France.

Taken to France by British paratroops of 6th Airborne, this pigeon was sent on the 130 mile journey back to England with the good news of the success of *Overlord.*

"All day it was hard to imagine how, whilst Londoners were calmly going about their business, not far away, there was fierce fighting going on the shores of France."

A. Brooke

Ver-sur-Mer. Casemate damaged by a shell.

Longues-sur-Mer, as it is today.

Omaha Beach. Unfinished casemate.

German defences.

202-514

THE ARTIFICIAL HARBOURS

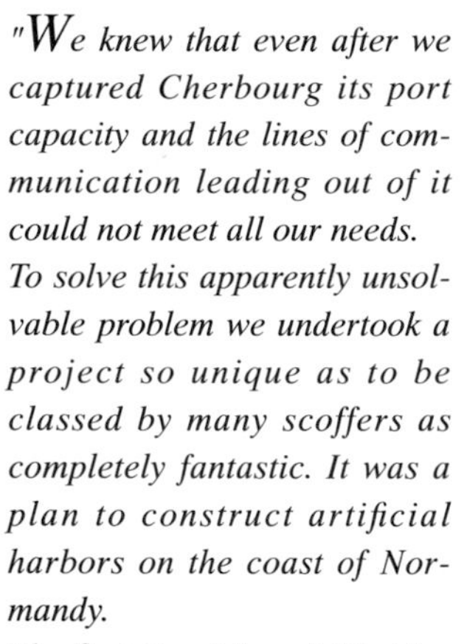

"We knew that even after we captured Cherbourg its port capacity and the lines of communication leading out of it could not meet all our needs.
To solve this apparently unsolvable problem we undertook a project so unique as to be classed by many scoffers as completely fantastic. It was a plan to construct artificial harbors on the coast of Normandy.
The first time I heard this idea tentatively advanced was by Admiral Mountbatten, in the spring of 1942. At a conference attended by a number of service chiefs he remarked, "If ports are not available, we may have to construct them in pieces and tow them in." Hoots and jeers greeted his suggestion but two years later it was to become reality."

D.D. Eisenhower

A CHALLENGE TO TECHNOLOGY

« They must float up and down with the tide; the anchoring problem must be mastered. Let me have the best solution worked out. Don't argue the matter. The difficulties will argue for themselves. »
Memo from W. Churchill to Vice-Admiral Mountbatten, May 10 1942.

In order to ensure supplies reached the expeditionary forces until such time as the harbour installations at Cherbourg were captured, the Allied planners had banked on setting up two artificial harbours, one off the American sector, the other off the British sector. Considered to be a deciding factor in the success of the operation in the bay of the Seine, this bold innovation had received the blessing of the top military authorities at the Quebec conference in August 1943. If truth be told, not only was setting up the *mulberry* harbours fraught with danger, the entire allied undertaking in the Channel was; however, the stakes were so high - the liberation of western Europe and beyond that, the elimination of Nazism - that the risks involved seemed justified.

The basic idea of prefabricated harbours was straightforward enough, involving the creation of a double area of water sheltered from the swell off the Calvados coast by constructing two artificial breakwaters. Within this sheltered water, unloading facilities would be provided with platforms linked by piers to dry land. Built in sections in Great Britain, the entire installation was to be towed across the Channel by tugs, the day after D Day. According to the scheme, each *mulberry* (code name for the synthetic harbours) was to be capable of handling 7,000 tons of stores and 1,250 vehicles per day, by D plus 15 (June 21), and to remain in service until the beginning of autumn 1944. At that time, it was thought that there would be a sufficient volume of maritime traffic going through whatever continental ports had by then been taken to make the *mulberries* redundant.

The first task was to find a solution to the three most awkward problems : creating sheltered anchorages, building quays for unloading purposes, and finally, linking the quays to the land. In answer to the first question as to how to set apart an area of calm water, it was decided to sink concrete blocks or caissons (known as Phoenixes)

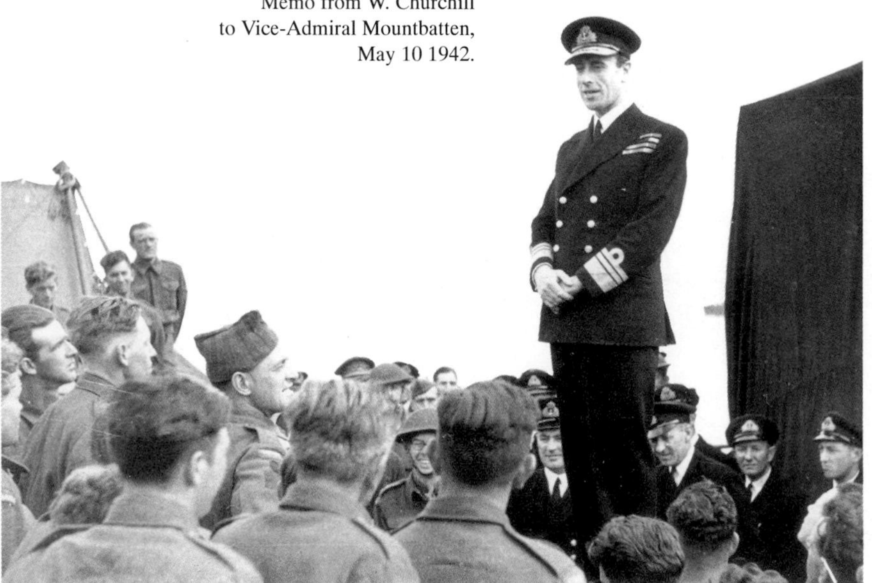

Vice-Admiral Mountbatten.

Omaha Beach. The *gooseberry* of the American artificial harbour initially consisted of 15 old ships. After the storm other ships were added to breach the gaps.

PREFABRICATED HARBOURS

on a line parallel to the shore and about 3/4 mile out. Behind this sea wall, small LCT-type landing craft and medium-sized cargo ships of the Liberty type could readily be accommodated. For the biggest ships with draughts requiring deeper waters to anchor in (over 30 feet at low tide), it was decided to add an outer anti-swell barrier, made up of elements of a new type called « bombardons », towards the open sea in front of the Phoenixes.

Inside the first sheltered anchorage, the one enclosed by concrete caissons, unloading quays or pierheads were to be installed. These were platforms of over two acres in area capable of following the movements of the tide by sliding up and down long piles resting on the sea bed. This ingenious system prevented unloading operations being interrupted at any time. The most delicate question to be settled was linking the wharves to dry land, because of the instability of the sea surface. After many fairly inconclusive tests and experiments, a system of relatively flexible metal roadways resting on steel caissons was adopted. Construction of the elements intended for the *mulberries* began in Great Britain in the autumn of 1943. The War Office (Army) was responsible for building the Phoenixes, the pierheads and floating roadways. The tasks of building the floating bombardons, directing towing operations and installing the artificial harbours off the Calvados coast were assigned to the Royal Navy. Rear-Admiral W.G. Tennant was put in charge as overall supervisor of the *mulberry* project by Admiral Sir Bertram Ramsay, commander-in-chief of the naval forces for Operation Overlord.

Like any conventional harbour, these synthetic harbours consisted of three main elements: breakwaters to act against the swell, wharves for unloading stores, and piers to connect the wharves to the land.

Sections of floating piers.

Artificial breakwaters

To protect the *mulberry* facilities against the swell, it had been arranged for two successive offshore barrages to be set up : a row of floating rafts (bombardons), and behind them, a breakwater made of sunken blockships extended by concrete blocks (Phoenix caissons).

The barrage of bombardons

Situated in front of the artificial harbours, this outer breakwater comprising a string of floating rafts, was the outermost protection of the harbour against the swell. The bombardons put into practice an original method of defence against the waves

Massive caisson under construction in a dock in England. Hiding these large structures from spotter planes of the *Luftwaffe* was a major headache. At no time did the German secret services suspect the use put to the Phoenixes (code name of the caissons).

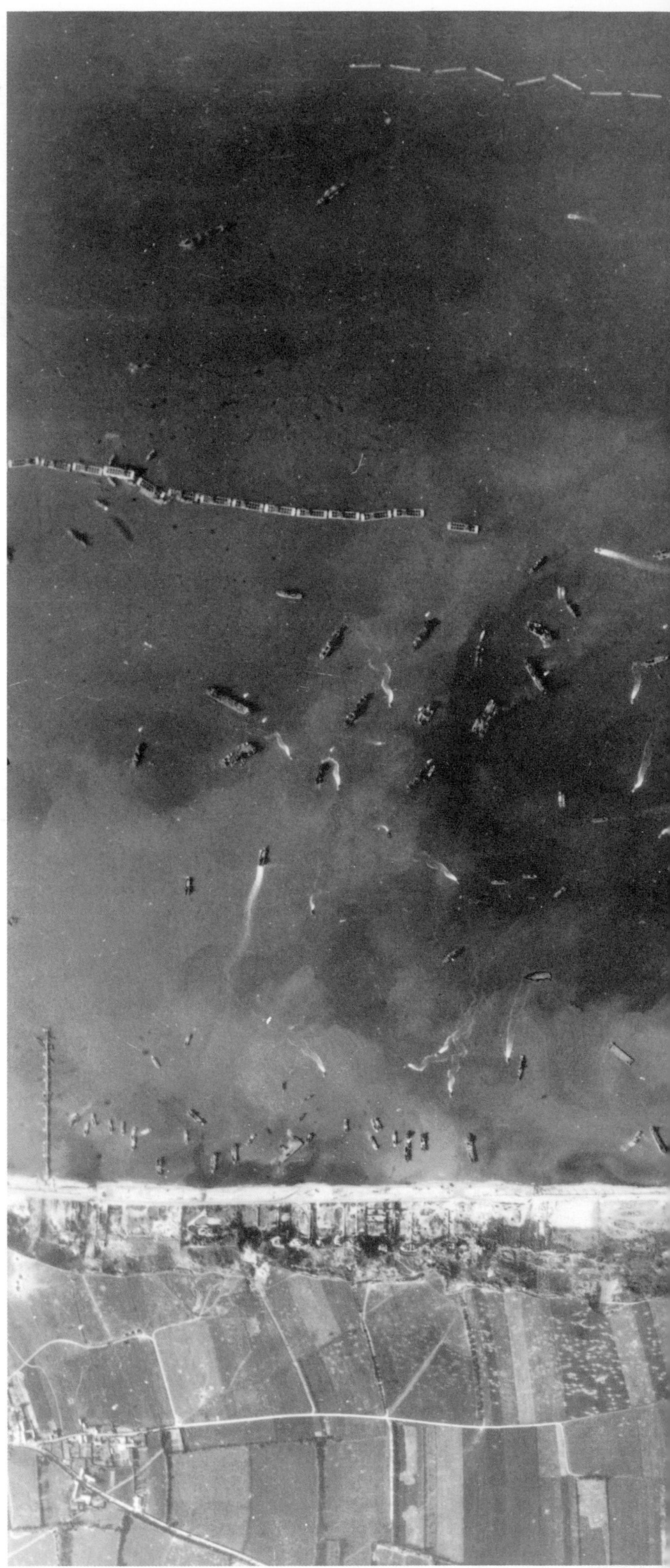

Omaha Beach

This excellent aerial photograph was taken on June 15, before the storm, at 28,000 feet by the US Air Force. In the middle of the picture is the beach codenamed *Dog Red* (Les Moulins, hamlet of Saint-Laurent-sur-Mer). To the right of Les Moulins, the beach extends towards Colleville *(Easy Green),* with the village of Vierville on the left. On this aerial photograph, the following can be seen, from top to bottom :

- the barrage of bombardons planted in a single row with several deep draught ships at anchor ;
- the breakwater comprising some fifteen carefully aligned Phoenixes ;
- the breakwater of blockships divided into several sections ;
- the LST wharf under construction, at the edge of the coastline, to the left ;
- the trace of a long anti-tank ditch barring entry to the wooded valley of the Ruquet, to the right ;
- the construction, on the top of the plateau, between Les Moulins and the valley of the Ruquet, of a campaign airfield (long white strip).

since the system relied on the principle whereby a heavy floating barrier hit side-on by a wave rolls and noticeably absorbs the energy of the swell. Tests carried out in force 6 winds, giving rise in the open sea to waves over 6 feet high, had shown that this height was reduced to 3 feet or less behind the chain of floats. The bombardons consisted of hollow cross-shaped metal caissons. Each 70-yard long and 30-foot high float drew 3 fathoms of water. Only watertight compartments in the upper branch of the cross ensured that it floated. The rest was filled with 2,000 tons of water, which gave this floating raft considerable inertia. The bombardons were strung together with a gap of about 15 yards between each section. This spacing was calculated to prevent waves surging through between the floats and reforming on the other side. Tests had confirmed that waves were flattened more effectively when the floating rafts were spread along two parallel lines; it was therefore recommended that this arrangement be adopted off the coast of Normandy. Anchored in deep water (approximately 10 fathoms), about 1 1/4 miles out to sea, before each of the

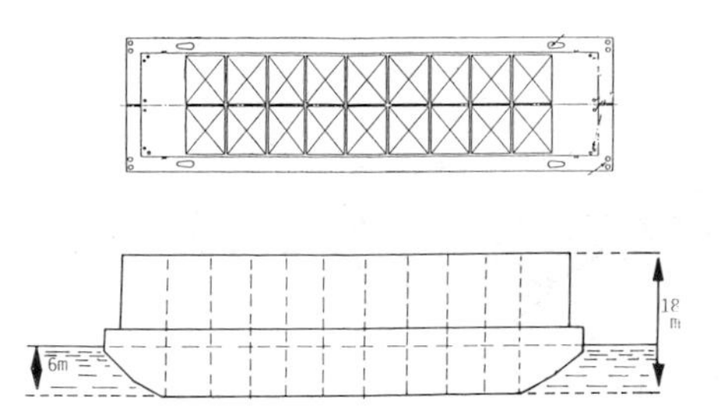

Arromanches. An aerial photograph of the breakwaters taken from directly above.

Arromanches. Building the *mulberry.* Taken from an angle, this aerial photograph clearly shows how the blockships and Phoenixes acted as breakwaters : the outer sea is rough, whereas the water is calm on the inside.

five assault beaches, this barrage was a total 3 1/2 miles long.

The breakwater of blockships

Behind the rows of bombardons, and off each of the landing beaches, it was intended that a breakwater should be laid by sending old ships ballasted with concrete to the bottom. These condemned ships got to be called blockships and the breakwater construction scheme was codenamed gooseberry. This was decided on by the Admiralty, on discovering that towing the Phoenixes across would be impossibly slow, so as to have an area of calm water in front of each of the five assault beaches as early as possible. Unlike the caissons, they had - at least most of them had - the great advantage of moving under their own steam. The first blockships would be put into position off the Normandy coast on the morning of June 7. This fleet, comprising cargo ships all having reached the end of their useful lives, some of them built at the end of the last century, and also a few downgraded warships, was laid on by Britain, the USA and the navies of the European allies. Placed end to end, the sixty or so blockships would have made a breakwater nearly 2 miles long.

Elements of the artificial port: breakwaters, quays on stakes and floating piers.

The *Phoenix* caissons

Sunk along the shoreline on the line of depths under 30 feet at low tide, the 147 concrete blocks built in Britain were designed to serve as a backbone to the breakwaters protecting the two artificial harbours. What they actually did was to extend and reinforce the two breakwaters of sunken blockships in place since the day after D Day at Saint-Laurent and

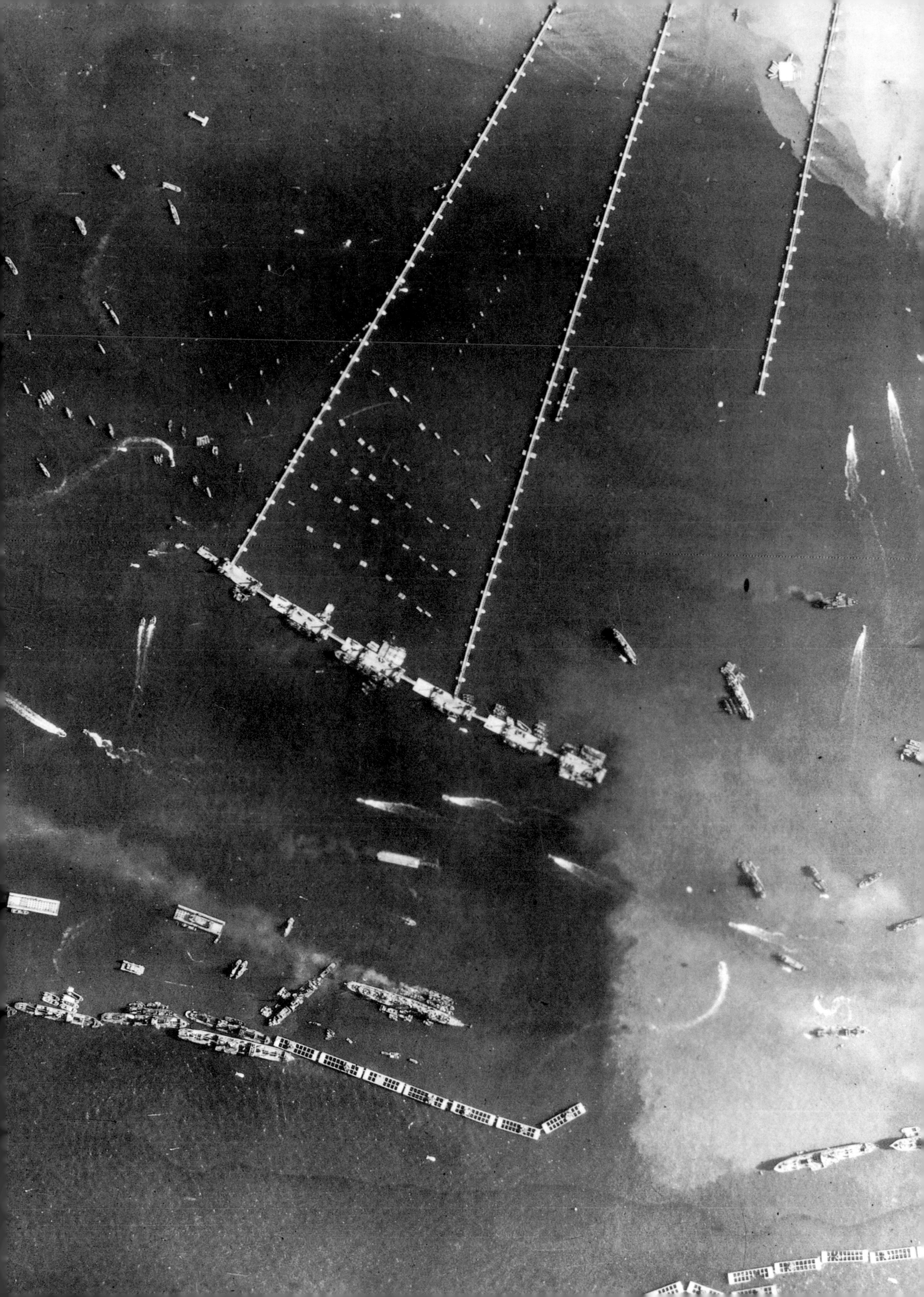

Arromanches. More caissons were to be used to consolidate piers set perpendicular to the coast.
The caissons, weighing anything between 1,600 and 6,000 tons came initially in six types designed to suit various depths of water. The largest blocks, which can still be seen today off Arromanches, were 200 feet long, 55 feet wide and 58 feet high (the height of a five-storey building). Each caisson was made up of two separate parts: a rectangular platform on which the block itself was fitted, divided into compartments that were partitioned off. Capable of floating but not of moving under their own steam, the caissons had to be towed across the Channel starting on June 7. Placed end to end they would have made a breakwater nearly 2 miles long.

The pierheads

At the heart of the vast artificial anchorage set apart by the caissons and blockships, the pierheads were set up. Used by vessels that could not run onto the sand, these quays were connected to the shore by piers. In order to offset the effects of the high levels of the powerful tides in the Bay of the Seine, by means of a system of pulleys and winches the platforms slid along four steel pylons approximately 100 feet high. The energy required to start these machines was supplied by generators powered by diesel engines. Thanks to a dummy sloping beach, some platforms enabled barges with opening bows like the LSTs to unload their vehicles directly onto the quay. These engines then came ashore using the floating piers.

The floating piers

Providing the link between the pierheads and dry land, the piers rested on floats placed at regular intervals. In order to absorb the deformation and twisting effects that the movement of the waves had on the assembly, telescopic spans were inserted at various points. In all about 10 miles of flexible roadway would be built and cross the Channel in 160-yard sections.

Filling a caisson.

Omaha beach. A quay on piles with (foreground) a pontoon shaped like an artificial beach enabling LST and LCT craft to come ashore and directly unload verhicles after lowering the ramp.

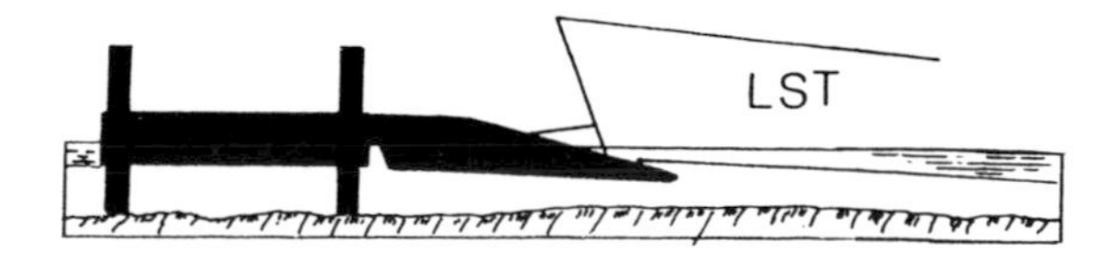

ASSEMBLING THE ARTIFICIAL HARBOURS

Phoenix caissons.

On June 6 1944, the greatest amphibious operation of the entire Second World War took place along the coast of lower Normandy. After disembarking nearly 140,000 men on the five assault beaches during the "Longest Day", the first priority of Admiral Ramsay was to ensure that supplies reached the units engaged on the mainland of Europe.

Supplying the allied expeditionary force

In order to meet the German counter-attack expected from D Day plus 4 (June 10), it was vital, as amphibious operations in Sicily and Italy had shown, that the Allied troops had their full fighting power at their disposal. Such an extremely tight schedule required in the absence of a port facility, special landing craft, at least some of which had to be able to cross the open sea and come straight ashore in less than three feet of water, and unload a steady flow of guns, ammunition, reinforcements and vehicles directly onto the sands of the beachhead by means of a ramp that opened out through the bows. In addition to these landing craft, larger deep draught merchant ships were also used to supply the troops in Normandy, as they had before in the Mediterranean. Unloading these cargo ships was performed out at sea by transferring cargoes onto hoppers (nicknamed "rhino-ferries") or amphibious trucks. Known as DUKWs, these craft shuttled back and forth between the large ocean-going ships at anchor behind the bombardons and the depots set up on the shore. It was with the intention of facilitating this transfer operation and the shuttle movements of the DUKWs that the Admiralty had requested that a *gooseberry* breakwater be constructed off each of the landing beaches, from June 7.

The five breakwaters

In order to set up the five breakwaters, as we have seen, it was intended to use about sixty old ships, that is a dozen on average per beach. In order to make the sinking procedure easier, the blockships had been ballasted with concrete and loaded with explosive charges just below the waterline on either side of the hull. Protecting Utah Beach, in the shape of a crescent, *gooseberry* n° 1 (ten blockships) was finally in position on June 13. Containing about fifteen ships, the Omaha breakwater (operation completed on June 10) would then, reinforced with Phoenix caissons, go to make up the artificial dyke for the *mulberry* to be. Off Arromanches and Courseulles where *gooseberries* 3 and 4 were sunk, the sinking operations were going to plan. The final barrage was set up off Hermanville and comprised nine blockships including the *Courbet*. As it happened, under daily attack from enemy artillery fire, aimed especially at the *Courbet,* which was bombed and torpedoed several times over, the anchorage next to the mouth of the Orne was abandoned by the Allies from June 20 until August 15. This loss would be offset by increased volumes brought ashore at the port of Courseulles, which had been captured almost intact.

Thanks to the breakwaters which made unloading possible round the clock and to Eisenhower's gamble allowing, starting on June 7, several LSTs to land side by side, in spite of the fact that these large vessels were easy targets for enemy bombers, tonnages brought ashore increased considerably in the week prior to the storm of June 19.

Once the two artificial ports came into service, the Allied command anticipated no major problems with resupplying.

Setting up the two artificial ports

Initially, the planning of the greatest towing operation in History had catered for daily departures to Normandy of thirty-five convoys on fifteen consecutive days. However, owing to a shortage of tugs, the Admiralty made a last minute decision to cut back the number of convoys and defer the finishing date for the *mulberries* by two or three weeks (i.e. D plus 21, June 27).

After the blockships, it was the turn of the bombardons, then the Phoenixes, pierheads, and sections of floating piers to head off for the coast of Normandy. Thanks to constant surveillance from the Royal Navy, losses due to enemy action during the Channel crossing were relatively slight. At Omaha, where things were going well and where they were going to show the British, they had a row of twenty-four bombardons, fifteen blockships for the *gooseberry,* thirty or so Phoenixes, a landing pier for LSTs and two quays on piles up and running by June 17. On June 18 (D plus 12), 11,000 men, 2,000 vehicles and 9,000 tons of supplies were brought ashore via the American *mulberry.* In

Assembling the piers.

spite of these figures, unloading in the American sector was at month's end still below expectations : 314,000 soldiers landed instead of 358,000, 40,000 vehicles out of 62,000, and 116,000 tons of supplies instead of 160,000. In the British sector too, in spite of the difficulties caused by the wind and tidal currents, they had their work cut out positioning the enormous concrete blocks that the tugs had to hold in place for the nearly half an hour it took to fill them. The day before the equinoctial storm, several piers and two quays on piles were already in place in the vast anchorage opposite Arromanches. In addition to the traffic passing through the two artificial harbours, there were also direct unloading operations on the beaches as well as those carried out in the smaller ports of lower Normandy (Courseulles and Port-en-Bessin, open to coasters from June 12).

By June 18 (D plus 12) there were on the continent, in the territorial base held along the Channel, a total of approximately 600,000 men, 100,000 vehicles and a week's rations and ammunition in advance. Petrol supplies were made by directly unloading it in jerry-cans on the harbour quays, on the beaches or through flexible semi-underwater hoses which connected tankers at anchor out to sea with storage tanks installed at Port-en-Bessin and Sainte-Honorine-des-Pertes where the fuel was stocked. In short, the day before the June 19 gale, the situation was by no means catastrophic: the landings kept a steady two days behind schedule. With the forthcoming opening of the two synthetic ports, there was reason to hope that something could be done to remove what backlog there was. However the storm temporarily put paid to such fine optimism.

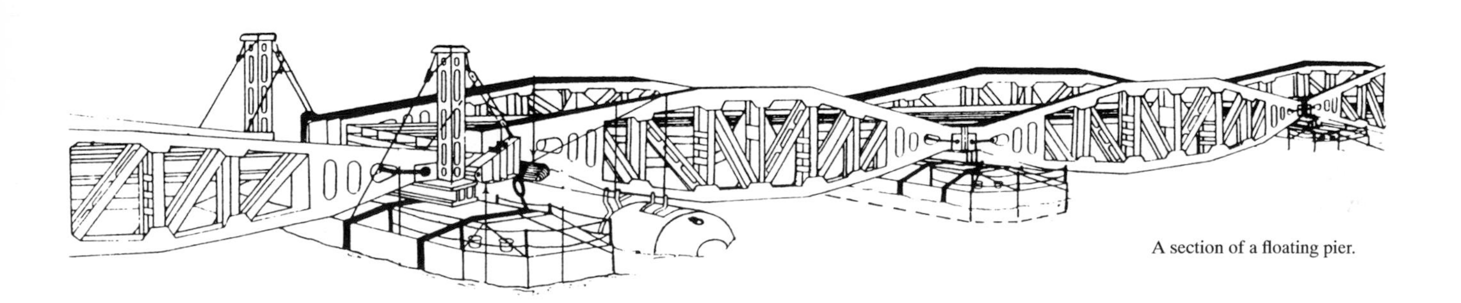

A section of a floating pier.

Arromanches.

THE GREAT STORM

Since the start of June, the weather was not all it might have been (fresh winds, reduced visibility and rough seas). Such poor weather conditions were to blame for the disappearance in the Channel of several sections of floating piers, the loss of two caissons, the capsizing of five tugs, and worst of all, delays to the beach landing programme.

Catastrophe at *Omaha Beach* (June 19-22 1944)

Following a slight improvement in the weather, on June 18, Admiral Tennant gave the go-ahead for twenty-four tugs to set off for the Calvados coast, each with a 160-yard section of floating pier in tow. When these heavy convoys had reached mid-Channel, the barometer suddenly dropped steeply and an unforecast gale blew up from nowhere whilst worrying troughs began to appear in the sea. Not designed to take any such strain, the moorings finally gave and nearly two miles of pier sank to the bottom, taking with them the best part of a dozen old tugs. The storm was to rage for the next seventy-two hours with occasional gusts of over 45 m.p.h. This was totally unheard of since the start of the century in the Channel for the time of year! In the gust, the rows of bombardons began to drift. These huge metal cases went berserk, causing tremendous injury to the Phoenixes. In the violence of the waves passing over the blockships, the quays on piles were shaken and even overturned at Omaha Beach after a collision with an LST.

On the morning of June 22, after three days of hell, the damage to the artificial harbours was enormous. The five breakwaters made of bombardons had been completely destroyed, several blockships had been displaced and many caissons were smashed. The manmade dykes had lost their protective value, as proven by the eight hundred craft that had gone aground in a great pile-up on the landing beaches. It was at Omaha, where the artificial harbour was by now in undescribable chaos, that the situation was the most catastrophic. The Allies had lost more material through bad weather in the space of just three days than since the start of D Day from attacks by the Germans. The main consequence of the gale was a considerable reduction in quantities unloaded in the landing sector on each of the next three days. The sudden drop in supplies of ammunition obliged the Allied command to put the brakes on certain operations already underway (the march on Cherbourg) and postpone other planned manoeuvres (the capture of Sainte-Honorine-la-Chardonnerette). This temporary halt imposed by the weather was used by Rommel to strengthen his

Effects of the storm.

Omaha beach, June 22 1944
This photograph, taken by a pilot in RAF 542 Squadron, shows the coastal sector code-named *Easy Green (*Les Moulins is on the right, the Ruquet valley on the left). Two sections of breakwater can be seen with blockships separated by a wide passage allowing the waves to reform in concentric rings inside the anchorage. One of the effects of the storm, scores of craft are piled up on the shore.

"The construction of the artificial harbor was a gigantic undertaking which was executed to perfection and it was nobody's fault if the mulberry facilities could not weather the storm. It was one of the worst gales ever seen in the Channel, you know. I was on a workshop craft in the middle of the harbor when the hurricane hit us and I can assure you it was very impressive. The hut we had built on the barge was blown away in the wind. At the same moment, whole sections of floating pier and bombardon were torn away and dashed against the shore. I had never seen such a tangle of twisted metal. It was a sad sight."

Testimony of American Lieutenant McEloy, who was in the harbour at Omaha when the storm broke.

defences and call in reinforcements from Brittany. However, apart from the arrival of these troops and a few batteries of artillery, the German command did not really exploit this unexpected advantage.

Recovery

In spite of the scale of the disaster, there was no question of losing hope on the Allies' side. It was a far cry from the mood at Dunkirk four years earlier! With the return of fine weather, the Allied command implemented a whole set of measures designed to set things to rights.
Apart from clearing up the beaches, repairing damaged landing craft, restoring the dykes at Omaha and Arromanches by the addition of several extra caissons, it was decided to increase the landings at the small harbours of lower Normandy (Courseulles, Port-en-Bessin, Grandcamp, Isigny, Saint-Vaast and Barfleur) ; on June 27, whilst American troops were capturing the port facilities at Cherbourg, ten days behind schedule, Eisenhower took the decision to drop any idea of reconstructing the Omaha *mulberry*. Meanwhile, the landings continued on the beaches of Saint-Laurent and Colleville, and, with this aim in mind, the *gooseberry* was strengthened. Any material not yet used for the American artificial harbour was transferred to Arromanches, where assembly was completed by the end of the first fortnight in July. Thanks to all these measures, by the end of June there were 850,000 men, 150,000 vehicles and 600,000 tons of supplies in Normandy. On July 8, six hundred landing craft that had gone aground during the storm were refloated on a big tide, with another hundred a fortnight later. On July 26, twenty-three days behind schedule, the first Allied convoy, made up of four liberty-ships, entered the large anchorage in Cherbourg harbour. From that day on, 12,000 tons of stores per day passed through Cherbourg and from mid-September 20,000 tons, after various work had been carried out. Fuel came ashore at the oil terminal at Port-en-Bessin or from England via an underwater pipeline (Pluto) into tanks at the port of Cherbourg.
In addition to Cherbourg and the artificial harbour at Arromanches, a not inconsiderable proportion of supplies were landed directly on the beaches in LSTs behind the breakwaters. At the end of July, the Americans broke all the records, landing 46,000 men and 8,000 vehicles in a single day on Utah and Omaha beaches alone. The beaches were doing better than Arromanches and Cherbourg put together. By the end of August (D plus 87),

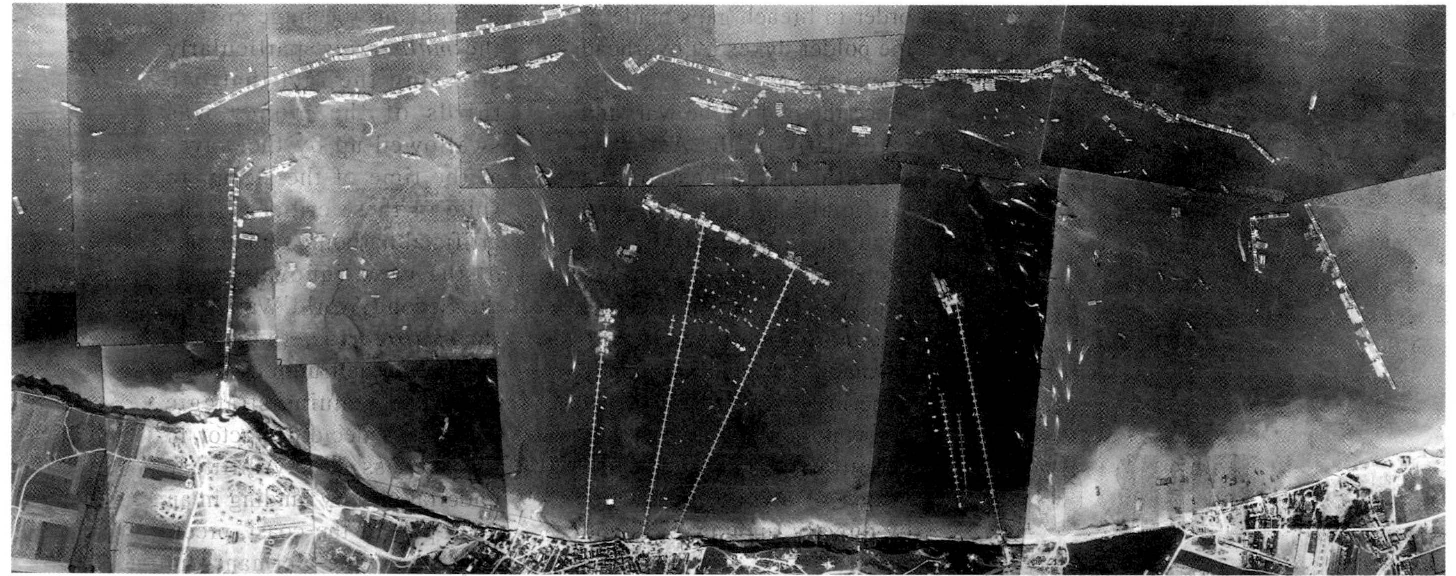

The artificial harbour at Arromanches on August 9 1944.

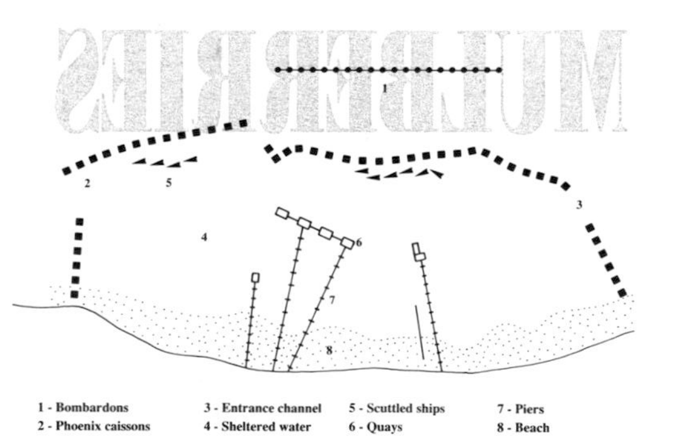

Plan of the Arromanches *Mulberry.*

whilst the Allies had reached the Somme, there were some 2,000,000 Allied soldiers, 500,000 vehicles of all kinds and 3,000,000 tons of supplies in France. Of this total, more than half had come directly ashore up the beaches, behind the breakwaters, about 20 per cent through the British artificial harbour, and an equal amount through the small Norman ports (Cherbourg plus the small fishing ports).

The closing of the beaches and harbours (November 1944)

With the coming of the bad weather, it became impossible to continue bringing supplies ashore on the beaches. Therefore, the Allied command took the decision to close the Normandy beaches in mid-November 1944. A month before, following the increase of traffic passing through Cherbourg and the capture of further facilities (Granville, Morlaix, Le Havre, Dieppe...) the Admiralty stopped using the small ports of lower Normandy, and these were handed over to the French authorities on November 9, 1944. The *mulberry* at Arromanches in turn was closed on November 19, and from the beginning of December, work began dismantling the pierheads and the floating piers. At the same time, several Phoenixes from the artificial harbour at Arromanches were towed to the island of Walcheren in

FOR OR AGAINST THE MULBERRIES

order to breach gaps made in the polder dykes by overhead bombing.
Since the end of the war, and particularly on the American side, the usefulness of the artificial harbours has been brought into question. Deprived of their *mulberry* because of the storm, the US command showed in the Channel, as it had previously done in Sicily and Italy, that it was possible to unload vast quantities of material in the shelter of a solid breakwater by directly running LSTs and a flotilla of DUKWs aground. Some had no compunction in qualifying the platforms that slid along the piles as sophisticated facilities and the floating roadways as complicated equipment that was too long to set up (assembly of the final pier at Arromanches was finished on July 19). During a post-war conference that created a scandal, British civil engineering specialists again brought up the huge cost of the *mulberries,* particularly stressing the fact that two thirds of the money was swallowed up by the waves at the time of the storm. In spite of these criticisms, the artificial harbours remain one of the great innovations of the Second World War. With the *mulberries,* the Allies held a unique trump card that produced genuine strategic surprise, a deciding factor in the success of any military undertaking. By landing in an open part of the coast, precisely where the Germans did not expect them, the Allies thwarted at a stroke the enemy's costly defensive system mainly concentrated around the large port installations, the natural gateways to the continent when approaching from the sea.
Without going so far as to claim to settle the issue, it is extremely difficult today to tell who, between the British and the Americans, performed the more incredible feat during the summer of 1944. The British designed, constructed, towed and assembled the harbour at Arromanches, the kingpin of Operation Overlord, whilst behind mere breakwaters, the Americans succeeded in landing many more vehicles, soldiers and ammunition directly onto the beaches than actually passed through the *mulberries...*

Arromanches. The *Phoenixes* today.

Arromanches in the 1950s.

THE BATTLE FOR NORMANDY

"The burnt-out skeleton of what used to be our town appeared in the pale early morning light. Fire ran along the streets, gradually moving from house to house with a loud crackling noise. And on this tragic awakening, the endless coils of a gigantic smoke-trail twisted away to the west, occasionally releasing half-burnt sheets of paper that landed sometimes miles further on with their derisory administrative texts still legible".

J. de Saint-Jorre

THE ALLIED PLAN

By the evening of D Day, the Allies had secured a foothold on the continent. The brutal and bloody throwing back into the sea promised by German propaganda had failed to materialize. This was a far cry from the muddle of *Jubilee!* "Overlord was in the bag". That was at least true for the phase of the plan involving the troop landings. Otherwise, the job was as yet far from finished: beachheads had to be consolidated, airfields captured or set up, mulberries had to be assembled, continental ports captured, fuel supplies ensured, reinforcements brought in, wounded and prisoners evacuated and, most of all, German counter-attacks by sea, land or air had to be repulsed.

Von Rundstedt and Rommel at Saint-Germain-en-Laye.

A spot of strategy

The battle plan for the Normandy campaign was a textbook affair drawn up by Montgomery, who had been appointed to command the American and British land armed forces for *Overlord.* The British forces, placed in the eastern sector of the beachhead, were given the task of drawing the German tank divisions. With this aim in mind, on the day after D Day, Montgomery's troops were to spearhead a thrust towards Caen giving the enemy to believe that the Allies' prime objective was to cross the Orne, head off towards Paris (working on the basis that "whoever holds Paris holds the country") and on to Germany itself. To keep up relentless pressure on the enemy and tie him down with the constant threat of breaking out, in such a way as to force him to commit the main part of his fighting reserves around the capital of lower Normandy, this was the task assigned to the British. By giving the Germans such a bone to chew on in the Caen sector, Montgomery made progress in the Cotentin easier for the Americans. On the mobile wing of the Allied armies, the Americans under Bradley were to cut off the peninsula, capture Cherbourg, break out southwards and, finally move up northwards to meet the British in order to encircle 7th German Army in a wide pocket.

Montgomery calls the tune

Based on the principle of alternating thrusts, the plan was that whenever one of the Allies encountered strong opposition, the other would launch an offensive in his sector in order to give the partner in difficulty some breathing space. Simple and easy to implement, Montgomery's project gave the Americans the better opportunity to show themselves to good effect. The British mission in June and July 1944 was basically to plug away at the enemy, to draw and hold the largest possible number of German divisions on the eastern flank. This was in contrast with the opposite flank where there were three times less German armoured vehicles, and the Americans had more room to manoeuvre. Reading the war communiques one gets the impression that Bradley and Patton's GIs were more combative than the Tommies and were the main victors in Normandy! As for the Germans, by over-committing themselves in the defence of their right flank, they fell straight into the trap that the victor at Alamein had laid for them. In the words of Eddy Bauer, the Swiss specialist of the tank war, in Normandy Rommel was to dance to Montgomery's tune.

Montgomery's Plan

"... once we had secured a good footing in Normandy, my plan was to threaten to break out on the eastern flank, that is in the Caen sector. By pursuing this threat relentlessly I intended to draw the main enemy reserves, particularly his armoured divisions into that sector and to keep them there - using the British and Canadian forces for this purpose. Having got the main enemy strength committed on the eastern flank, my plan was to make the break-out on the western flank - using for this task the American forces under General Bradley. This break-out attack was to be launched southwards, and then to proceed eastwards in a wide sweep up to the Seine about Paris. I hoped that this gigantic wheel would pivot on Falaise. It aimed to cut off all the enemy forces south of the Seine, the bridges over that river below Paris having been destroyed by our air forces."

B.L. Montgomery

Bradley, Montgomery.

THE CAPTURE OF CHERBOURG June 1944

We may consider the long battle of Normandy (June 6 - August 21 1944) in three main stages, each roughly coinciding with a month of the summer of 1944. June was devoted to cutting off the Cotentin peninsula and to the American conquest of the *Festung* of Cherbourg. After a long period of slow progress both in the bocage and in the plain, on the opposite flank, July brought three pieces of good news: the capture of Saint-Lô, the liberation of Caen and the break-out of Patton's army towards Avranches. The month of August was filled with murderous fighting and after almost 80 days of struggle saw the end of the battle with the encircling of the 7th German Army in the Falaise Gap.

On the evening of June 6, the Anglo-Americans had not achieved all their objectives and only two British beaches *(Gold* and *Juno)* had been joined up. The first task of the troops was thus to link up the different lodgements in a single bridgehead in order to prevent the Germans counterattacking down the corridors separating the assault beaches, as they had tried to do between *Sword* and *Juno,* and through their skill and the superiority of their tanks, picking off the Allied forces one by one. On June 7, the British troops who had landed on *Gold Beach* entered Bayeux (the first town in France to be liberated) and headed west to meet the Americans who had come ashore at Omaha. On the way, three miles west of Arromanches, they captured the garrison of the Longues-sur-Mer shore battery in the early hours without a shot being fired. For their part, the Americans of *Omaha,* whilst seeking to make contact with the troops that came ashore to their right at *Utah,* sent out reconnaissance parties in the direction of Port-en-Bessin in order to link up with the British. This was achieved a few hours after the capture of Port-en-Bessin by the 47th Commando of the *Royal Marines.* Thus, by June 8, the Allies held a continuous forty-mile long strip of shore along the Calvados coastline extending from the Orne estuary to the Vire estuary. With Courseulles taken almost intact by the Canadians, Montgomery had two ports to unload supplies for the Allied Expeditionary Force. In the first of a series of visits, Churchill landed at Courseulles on June 12, and two days later, it was General de Gaulle's turn to set foot on French soil and make a few speeches, followed, on the 16th, by the king of England. On June 12, D+6, the Americans of Omaha crossed the river Vire and established contact with troops under General Collins who had come ashore at *Utah.* With this further link-up, the beachhead was now 50 miles long and the front was about twelve miles deep, with the deepest penetration towards Saint-Lô and

A view of the range-finding station at Longues-sur-Mer.

Port-en-Bessin, captured on June 7.

BAYEUX

De Gaulle in Bayeux.
Opposite page: Bayeux. June 44.

Caumont. That same day, after fierce fighting against the soldiers of General von der Heydte's 6th Parachute Regiment, the Americans captured Carentan and also the heavy artillery battery at Saint Marcouf-Crisbecq. With these exploits behind them, they headed off towards Barneville, a small seaside town on the west coast of the Cotentin, straight across from *Utah,* and reached on June 18. Having thus cut off the northern sector of the peninsula, Bradley ordered Collins to start moving up towards Cherbourg. The previous day at Margival near Soissons, Rundstedt and Rommel had had a stormy interview with Hitler about the situation in Normandy. After a hardfought battle, Montebourg fell on June 19, then Valognes, in ruins, two days later. Cherbourg was now only twelve miles away. It was at this moment that the US forces laid hands on several dozen secret weapon (V1 and V2) launching sites.

"I have just travelled about twenty miles across the liberated sector of France before coming to the main street in Bayeux. The whole town has put out flags. The townspeople are showering flowers on our soldiers, but they are now paying special attention to the traitors who collaborated with Germany. The population is attacking the leaders of the collaborationist gang. An angry crowd is dragging the leader of the antibolchevist legion through the streets of the town. He is a stocky chap with grey hair. He is panic-stricken, tries to parry the blows that are raining down on him from all sides. A young French partisan, armed with a rifle, is trying to hold back the crowd. A few moments before, the inhabitants of Bayeux had grabbed a member of the collaborationist police. This is how the people of France, or all at least what I have seen of them today are letting of steam. They do so by showing how glad they are to see us, and especially by giving a free rein to four years of suppressed hatred, hatred of the Germans and their accomplices."

British Journalist

SAINT-MARCOUF

A heavy gun casemate at Saint-Marcouf-Crisbecq.
Opposite page: fighting in the bocage of the hinterland.

CARENTAN

Take-off runway in the bocage of the Cotentin.

GI in battledress.

The liberation of Carentan.

MONTEBOURG BRICQUEBEC

Above: the ruins of Montebourg.
Opposite: Bricquebec.

VALOGNES

Very early on, the Germans proceeded to requisition the best dwellings in the town for the purpose of setting up offices and *Wehrmacht* headquarters as well as the technical departments of the Todt Organization responsible for building the Atlantic Wall fortifications. Having taken over the beautiful residences, they soon made further demands on food supplies, draught animals and all kinds of fatigue-duty.

Despite the leaflets dropped by Allied planes inviting the population to take refuge in the surrounding countryside, very few inhabitants had evacuated the town at the time of the invasion. Considering that Valognes was an important rail and road communications centre where, as at Montebourg, enemy rearguard action was liable to hold up the troops' advance on Cherbourg, the American command proceeded to a preliminary bombing of the town, on June 6. After the Alleaume quarter, it was the turn of the station area and the town centre to come in for a real pounding in the days that followed. Almost a tenth of the population disappeared under this deluge of bombs, and nearly a thousand buildings. By June 21 1944, Valognes was nothing but a mass of ruins, as a local historian explains.

Clearing the ruins with a bulldozer.

"On June 6, the fire brigade and volunteer helpers organized the picking up of the wounded and administered first aid. But very quickly a second wave disrupted their attempts. In this dreadful chaos, many owed their lives to those who dug them out of the rubble where they were buried... The centre of Valognes was completely flattened by the bombs and reduced to a smoky mass. The survivors could save nothing from their ruined houses, for even the ruins were on fire... The church was reduced to a heap of stones, the fine wood work and the bells all disappeared in the rubble. Anything that was more or less falling over finally did so with the passage of the tanks."

Nadine Bois
"Valognes ou la volonté de vivre"

A British flak battery.
Following page: The Americans in the Cotentin peninsula.

"The unfolding of the battle of Normandy, now in progress, clearly demonstrates the nature of the enemy's intentions. He means to secure a deep beachhead, between the Orne and the Vire, which will then serve as a springboard for launching a powerful offensive in northern France, probably towards Paris. The enemy is seeking to isolate the Cotentin peninsula and to capture Cherbourg as quickly as possible, in order to have a large port capable of unloading vast quantities of equipment."

Rommel

Vl and V2

V1 and V2 installations in the Cotentin

Being relatively close to the southern coast of Britain (Portsmouth is only 90 miles from Cherbourg), in 1944 the Cotentin peninsula was crammed with German military installations. In addition to the radar and radionavigation stations at La Hague and the Val de Saire, south of Cherbourg, there were many densely packed secret weapon (V1 and V2) launching sites. These mystery installations were captured by troops under General Collins, on their way up to Cherbourg.

The pilotness plane - V1

The V1 was a small plane, simple and cheap to manufacture in the underground factories of the Reich; it was 25 feet long with an 18 foot wingspan and weighed roughly 2 tons including its 2000 lb warhead. The propulsion mechanism placed over the fuselage comprised an 11'6" long exhaust pipe containing a jet engine. Flying at speeds of approximately 375 mph and altitudes from 2000 to 2800 feet, the V1 was aimed directly at a town in southern England, launched from a ramp, reaching its target after a flight lasting about twenty minutes. The V1 was launched by means of the catapult procedure already in use on aircraft carriers. In the first installations at least, both ramp and catapult were protected by two concrete walls, as can be seen in the photograph opposite. Apart from the ramp, a V1 launching station comprised roughly ten other buildings (galleries serving as stores for the plane, an assembly area, concrete shelters for storing the chemicals required to operate the catapult, explosive stores, fine-tuning workshop, ranging station...). Not a single V1 was fired from the Cherbourg peninsula. The first was

V1 launching ramp.

A V1 after a take-off error.
Opposite page: ramp at Brécourt.

V1 launch site at La Sorellerie (Manche).

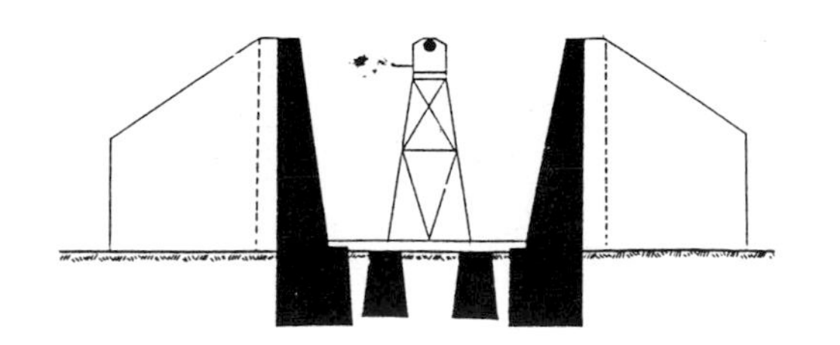

launched from ramps sited in the north of France during the night of June 12 to 13 a week after the invasion.

The V2 rocket

The V2 rocket was a revolutionary device 15 yards high and weighed 13 tons at take-off including 9 tons of fuel and oxidant. The fuel used was methanol (5,070 lb) and 14,770 lb of liquid oxygen provided the oxidant required to work the missile's engine insofar as its flight path took it for most of the time ınto empty space beyond the upper layers of the atmosphere. Each rocket carried a ton of explosive placed in the nose of the missile. In order to escape the pull of gravity, the rocket engine, which got up to 700,000 HP, was powered by a mighty turbopump of an entirely original design. A genuine miracle of technology, this turbopump was capable of discharging nearly 450 lb of fuel per second into the combustion chamber! A long-range rocket designed for bombing Britain's large cities, the V2 was the first ballistic missile in history and the ancestor of all modern rockets whether Saturn or Soyuz. Under the action of its propellent the V2 had an absolutely vertical take-off position. There was no question of any ramp. Propulsion was ensured through the extremely high expulsion rate of the liquids

V2 rocket at blast-off.

Diagram of the V2 base at Brix.

contained in the tanks. With an initial thrust of 25 tons, it reached the speed of sound in less than half a minute. At an altitude of 30 miles, and still climbing, the rocket began to level out in the programmed direction. A minute after blast-off, 30 miles up, when the missile was flying through the stratosphere, its speed was close to 3,750 mph, five times the speed of sound. After a ground station cut off fuel combustion, the missile carried on its upward movement, then fell down onto its objective at a speed of 2,200 mph.
The entire flight lasted under 300 seconds. After burying itself several yards into the ground, due to the effect of its speed, the diabolical missile would explode, producing a crater about forty yards in diameter.

Owing to the number and complexity of the operations to be carried out before launching, the German high command had built special bunkers in northern France and in the Cherbourg peninsula. In the Cotentin, a giant bunker was constructed in the village of Brix, south of Cherbourg. Designed to house a hundred missiles as well as the chemicals required for launching, this vast installation was never completed following Allied bombing raids. The first V2 rocket fired against London was launched from Holland, on September 8 1944.

A V2 on its special carriage with hydraulic lifting system.
Opposite: V2 rocket launching base at Brix.

CHERBOURG

Aerial view of Cherbourg harbour (USAF).

Naval battle at Cherbourg

Faced with fierce resistance from certain fortified positions and General von Schlieben's refusal to capitulate, General Collins, commanding VIIth US Corps, requested the help of the *US Navy* in order to neutralise the large coastal batteries *(York, Brommy, Hamburg ...)* installed along the northern coast of the Cotentin. Following this appeal for help, a naval fleet was assembled in Portland, not far from Weymouth, and placed under the command of Admiral Deyo. Divided into two groups, the fleet detailed to bombard the German defences at Cherbourg and the surrounding area included 5 heavy American battleships *(the Tuscaloosa, Texas, Arkansas, Quincy and Nevada)* and two British battleships (the *Glasgow* and the Enterprise). This group was accompanied by a dozen destroyers, a flotilla of mine-sweepers as well as air cover. Beginning at noon or thereabouts, on Sunday June 25, the fighting would last roughly 3 hours. After the *York battery* (Querqueville) had opened fire with its 4170-mm guns placed in casemates, hitting the *Glasgow* but without causing any serious damage, the *US battleship Nevada* began returning fire with supporting fire from the *Tuscaloosa* and the *Quincy*. Using its large modern 355-mm calibre guns with a range of 44,000 yards, the *Nevada* scored one direct hit without silencing the three other German pieces. In its turn, the *Glasgow* joined in the fun and tried to silence the 4150-mm gun battery installed at Castel-Vendon, about eight miles west of Cherbourg. Meanwhile, the destroyers were busy knocking out various strongholds along the shore whose position had been indicated to them by General Collins (works at the Fort de l'Est, the Jetée des Flamands, the Arsenal...). Whilst group 1, placed under the command of Admiral Deyo, was engaged in neutralising defences situated west of the port of Cherbourg, group 2 (Admiral Bryant, *US Navy*) had been detailed to silence the *Brommy* (Tourlaville) and *Hamburg* (Fermanville) batteries. If Brommy was the twin sister of Castel-Vendon, Hamburg, on the other hand, with its four 240-mm guns with a range of twenty-five miles, was the largest artillery emplacement in the whole Bay of the Seine. In the absence of the *Nevada* which had still not had it out with *York,* the task fell to the *Arkansas,* a battleship built before the First World War, and the *Texas* of silencing the *Hamburg's* guns, placed in emplacements that were still unfinished in June 1944. Using their old 14-inch (355-mm) and 12-inch (305-mm)

US *Quincy*-type cruiser.

Americans watching Cherbourg from the top of the fort at Le Roule.

guns with a range of a dozen or so miles, the *Texas* and the *Arkansas* showered the artillery positions at Fermanville totally destroying a gun, but not without the German cannons in turn hitting a US battleship and several destroyers. In total, at around 3 p.m., by the time Admiral Deyo gave the signal for the return to Portland, the *Texas* had fired 206 355-mm shells, the *Arkansas* 58 305-mm shells and the 5 escorting destroyers 552 127-mm shots. Although it did not completely silence the German coastal batteries, the naval bombardment, combined with the aerial bombardment and violent artillery fire from the army, according to Admiral Krancke and General Schlieben had a disastrous effect on the morale of the Cherbourg garrison. Coming in behind this deluge of steel, the American troops entered the town on the following day and in the afternoon of June 26 obtained the unconditional surrender of von Schlieben and Admiral Hennecke at around 3 p.m. After 1467 days of German occupation, Cherbourg was free again. And the battle for Cherbourg figures in all the official American histories as one of the big naval battles of the Second World War and more particularly as an illustration of the superiority of on-board artillery over land-based artillery.

General von Schlieben at General Collins' H.Q.

The surrender of General von Schlieben

On learning that General Karl von Schlieben, commander of the Festung Cherbourg (Fortress Cherbourg), had just repeated Marshal von Paulus's gesture of capitulation in Stalingrad, Hitler was boiling with rage: "It must be ensured that the most valiant officers are placed in command of the fortresses and not such braggarts as the type that we had at Cherbourg who made a boastful announcement, went up to the front line and the most advanced bunker to wait until the enemy arrived and then promptly raised the white flag. When the enemy said to him: "How can you reconcile your honour with the fact that you made such an announcement?" he just shrugged his shoulders... After remarking that it is the quality of the individual that counts and not his rank, Hitler had this to add on the subject of this gang of high-ranking officers: "They are nothing but cowards who have been educated in such a way that they consider it perfectly natural... for others to make sacrifices whilst they themselves refuse to get stuck in because they already have an eye in the other direction, saying to themselves: what can happen to us? We shall be taken prisoner, we shall be treated according to our rank, especially those of us who are of noble extraction!". This is intolerable and that is why we must review the list of all commanders in place. We must learn our lesson from the Cherbourg affair!... We are behaving like the Italians in acclaiming these miserable and spineless cowards as if they were heroes..."

Helmut Heiber

Cherbourg. Underground passage used as von Schlieben's command post.

VIVE DE GAULL
VIVE LES ALLI
VIVE LA REP BLIQUE

The French try their traitors

"The natives of Normandy are a conservative, orderly people. When the Germans were driven out of the Norman towns by the Allies, the Frenchmen showed none of the violence against collaborationists which the rest of the world expected. Even when dealing with out-and-out traitors, the Normans kept within the law. In the first trial of collaborationists to take place on French soil since the beginning of the invasion, a Cherbourg military tribunal tried and convicted two miserable young Frenchmen who had spied on Allied troops for the Germans. Instead of being executed, the two spies were sentenced to life imprisonment. The defense argued that they were too young to have grown to maturity under any influence save that of Germans and the Vichy French. Few of the Normans were outright collaborationists and most of these went along with the retreating Germans. The majority of the people remained peacefully at their jobs without causing the enemy any trouble. Whether this orderly return to normal life would be repeated in other parts of France was another matter. In places where resistance against the Germans and the collaborationists has been strong, bad feeling and bloodshed among the French is more likely to occur.
The smooth conduct of the Cherbourg trial, however, illustrated the fact that the process of re-establishing legal government in Normandy is proceeding. General Eisenhower's G-5, or Civil Affairs division, has made no attempt to set itself up as an independent governing authority, left French government to the French. For their part, the French have accepted the provisional government of Charles de Gaulle."

Life, July 1944

Cherbourg. Arresting the traitors.

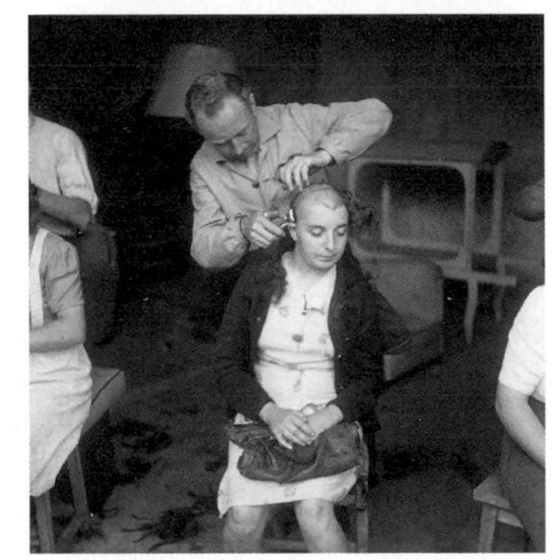

Headshaving operation.
Opposite: July 14 at Cherbourg.

In total, by the end of June, the Americans had lost almost 20,000 men, but they had finally seized the installations of a big continental port even though more than a week behind schedule. The trouble was that the US Navy had been prepared to find the port in a semi-demolished state, but what met their eyes was far worse than their worst fears: dynamited wharves, road beds cluttered with blockhouses or broken up, railway lines ripped out, unusable docks cluttered with wrecks, railway terminal and sheds in ruins, cranes thrown down at the foot of the wharves, mines and all kinds of traps placed in the mud of the docks or under rolls of barbed wire to prevent them being defused... It was an utter disaster and an apocalyptic sight. It took nearly a month to clear the docks, to refloat over a hundred wrecks, repair the breaches in the quays, complete minesweeping operations, re-establish the roadways and railways, reconstruct the working tools (lifting and handling equipment...). In short, it was almost the end of July before the first liberty-ship could enter the sheltered water of the large port in the Cotentin. Meanwhile, whatever could not be unloaded at Cherbourg was therefore brought ashore at Arromanches or directly onto the beaches from the large LST.

Cherbourg. Unloading heavy *matériel.*

PLUTO

The question of fuel supplies, a vital one for any modern army, took first place in the *Overlord* plan along with the capture of airfields and continental ports. It must be said that the fuel requirements (petrol for the vehicles, kerosene for the airforce, diesel fuel for the ships engines) were colossal, estimated at 15,000 tons per day on D+41 (July 15). So as to avoid any shortage for the 200,000 vehicles that would be present by that time on the bridgehead, and have advance supplies equivalent to a fortnight's average consumption, meant unloading more than 500,000 tons of petroleum products on the Normandy coast between June 6 and July 15 in the face of enemy counter-attacks. In order to pull off this tour de force, the chiefs-of-staff decided upon several supply systems. During the first ten days following the assault, with no installations as yet available, fuel was unloaded directly onto the beaches in metal jerry-cans from LCT that ran aground. Meanwhile, the navy set up an anchorage for petrol-tankers off Sainte-Honorine-des-Pertes connected by two sealines (flexible piping laid on the sea bed) to tanks sited on the rising ground of the Mont Cauvin, a few miles to the rear. Nearby at Port-en-Bessin an oil terminal was set up along the piers also to feed the Mont Cauvin oil-tanks through rigid pipes. Known as the *minor system,* this initial installation was shared by the Americans and the British. This initial means of supply was scheduled to be phased out on July 15 and replaced either by the so-called *major system* installations in the port of Cherbourg. With a higher flow rate, the major system was simultaneously fed by large oil-tankers anchoring at the Querqueville pier terminal used by the French navy before the war and by an undersea pipe-line nicknamed PLUTO. Owing to the scale of the destruction of the port installations, the first tanker did not come alongside the pier until July 25, a month after the capture of the port. PLUTO was a system that had been definitively abandoned by the Americans in December 1943 because of the difficulties involved in setting it up; the process of laying it across the Channel between the Isle of Wight and Cherbourg, a distance of approximately 60 miles, was behind schedule from the outset. In actual fact, this operation of unwinding ten flexible pipelines along the sea bottom had never been previously performed by the team. In theory, each tube was to

Pluto pipelines.

transfer 300 tons a day and according to the initial plan, the first pipe should have reached Cherbourg by D+12 (18 June). The belated capture of the fortress, bad weather and the slowness of the clearing up operations in the Cherbourg area meant that PLUTO was only pressurised at the beginning of August, six weeks late. This delay meant there was a shortfall of over 100,000 tons of fuel, which did not however cause too many problems since the Americans' progress in the bocage was slow and hence their fuel consumption was lower than expected. The late implementation and under-performance of the *major system* due to problems with PLUTO obliged the high command to increase unloading operations at the Port-en-Bessin terminal, in the small harbours (Courseulles) and especially on *Utah* and *Omaha* beaches. With the movement of the front it became necessary to extend the network of pipelines from the storage pool at Cherbourg first southwards in the direction of Avranches and the Loire. Then early in August, General Bradley changed the initial path and moved PLUTO towards Paris and the Seine. Nearly 7,500 sappers of the American army with the help of 1,500 German prisoners-of-war were requisitioned to complete the earth-removing and welding work. In actual fact, the task was not always carried out properly and, rather than lose time digging trenches across fields, which slowed down progress due to the slowness of mine-clearing operations, the pipes were simply placed in the ditches lining the roads. The result was that the pipes were subjected to strain and deformation and finally bursts. On top of these troubles, the official American historian stresses the lack of public spirit shown by the local population who had no qualms about bursting the pipes and helping themselves. For this reason the valves had to be shut off on several occasions and sentries posted along the pipeline. After the capture of the port installations at Le Havre, Dieppe, Boulogne and Antwerp and the laying of a second undersea pipeline between Dungeness and Boulogne (8 pipes delivering a total 3,500 tons per day), it became pointless to extend the Cherbourg pipelines. Having just reached the other bank of the Seine, south of Paris, PLUTO would go no further.

Pipeline on the road to Escures.
Opposite: Starting point of Pluto in Cherbourg.

CAEN
July 1944

Whilst the Americans were fighting a difficult battle in order to enter Cherbourg, at the other end of the front, following their failed attempt at capturing Villers-Bocage in mid-June, the British were preparing to launch a new offensive.

Epsom

Codenamed *Epsom,* the objective of this powerful attack spearheaded by 60,000 men with 400 armoured vehicles in support was to capture Caen and its airfield. In reality, without air support due to bad weather, the encircling movement around Caen from the west was quickly contained by the *Panzer* divisions and the airfield at Carpiquet which the RAF wanted so badly stayed out of reach. If Epsom was a fiasco, the *Gegenangriff* (counter-attack) launched in the Caen sector by the former *Panzergruppe West,* since renamed 5. *Panzerarmee* (5th Tank Army), fared no better. Through the combined action of the tactical air-force and the naval artillery, the *Panzerdivisionen* were literally nailed to the spot. Gunfire from the big 406-mm guns of the battleships *Rodney* and *Nelson* was particularly accurate and devastating. The deflagration of a shell of this calibre exploding near a 60-ton tank was so powerful that it was capable of overturning it. Basically, what the

Outflanking Caen on the West
EPSOM

"There still remained an outside chance of capturing the town by outflanking it on the west. It was in this direction that the British cannonades were most often to be heard, in relatively short bursts followed by long periods of silence. The land would shake for two or three hours, then calm would return, and this rythmn bore no resemblance to the almost continuous thundering at Verdun or in the Somme. There was no shortage of quiet days. At other times, there were tank encounters, a short deafening noise. All this was characteristic of this trenchless war which at the same time was a hand-to-hand affair with ambushes in the hedges and patrols of camouflaged men, the German-lizards enveloped in their camouflage canvas, the British with painted faces. On a large-scale map, the front appeared to be unbroken... In the complex reality of the countryside it was not... This battle for the west of Caen was fought to a certain extent in open terrain, near the airfield and of the village of Carpiquet, but for the most part in bocage country between the upper Seulles and the Odon rivers.

Henri Contamine
Memories of the Battle for Caen

Map-making.

Germans had suffered the previous summer at Gela in Sicily or Salerno in Italy was happening all over again in Normandy. In spite of the failure of *Epsom,* Montgomery had the consolation of knowing that Rommel had risen to the bait. After all, the former victor at Alamein was holding the main part of the enemy forces around Caen and in the vicinity of Hill 112, the ridge of high ground separating the valley of the Odon from the Orne valley. It only needed the war correspondents to accuse the commander-in-chief of lacking in offensive spirit and in their articles to worry over the poor territorial gains achieved by the British in their sector. As Bradley wrote, Monty could not justify himself without giving away the secret strategy of his manoeuvre. The Germans had to be convinced that the Allies' main effort was against Caen.

British airfields in Normandy

Maintaining air superiority over the beachhead was a prerequisite for the success of the Allied operation. Also, the capture of the French airfields as well as the creation of landing strips figured high on the list of objectives for the armies under Eisenhower. Three days after the beach assault, there were 11,000

The plain around Caen. Building an airstrip.

sappers equipped with 2,600 vehicles in the British sector alone ready to set up twenty airstrips in the plain of Caen.
The plan had provided for an emergency landing strip, on the evening of D Day, two others for refuelling and munitions supplies by D+3, 10 by D+15 and about forty by the end of August. Unfortunately, the area planned for the installation of the airstrips, namely the vast belt of open, flat country between the Paris road and the Falaise road remained under enemy control until the beginning of August. Also, the RAF only had the infrastructures established in the narrow bridgehead lying between the Channel and the front line. All these airstrips were oriented in an east-west direction, were too short and too close to one other, and were dangerous both on take-off and on landing due to the volume of air traffic and the consequent risks of collision.
Three types of ground installation were planned: *Emergency landing strips* (ELS, 550 yards long), the *Rearming and refueling strips* (RRS), and lastly the *Advanced landing grounds* (ALG) whose strips were 1100 or 1550 yards long and 36 yards wide. With powerful earthmoving equipment (bulldozers, scrapers, mechanical diggers, steamrollers...) at their disposal, the air force

sappers could build ALGs (airstrips covered with a square-meshed steel netting, access roads, aircraft parking lots, depots, workshops, barracks for the aircrews) inside a week. Covering a surface area of roughly 500 acres, each ALG required for its construction approximately 800 tons of materials (rolls of netting, stakes, clips...) i.e. the equivalent of 400 lorry-loads!
Codenamed B1, the first landing strip set up by the British in Normandy was sited in the village of Asnelles, on June 7. It was an emergency airfield designed to receive aircraft in difficulty that could not make it back to base in England. The first aircraft to use it was a Spitfire, on June 8, at around 1.00 p.m. In the days following, the sappers began construction of B2 at Bazenville, B3 at Sainte-Croix-sur-Mer, B4 at Beny, B5 at Camilly and B6 at Coulombs. B3 was the first proper airfield set up in France by the RAF, and had two parallel runways used on June 11 by British fighters and, from June 13, by two fighter groups belonging to the Free French Air Forces (Alsace and Ile-de-France). Built between June 10 and 16, the Coulombs airfield with its two 1,060 yard strips was the biggest British airfield in Normandy. As early as June 17, three squadrons of Typhoons landed at Coulombs followed, a few days later, by sixteen Dakotas loaded with nearly 500 tons of matériel for the big airfield at Lantheuil. Coulombs and Lantheuil had required the opening of two new quarries (at Vaux-sur-Seulles and Cully), those at Orival and Creully having become inaccessible due to the heavy traffic on the roads.
Landing strips were built at Plumetot, Martragny, Amblie, Villons-les-Buissons, and at Saint Aubin d'Arquenay. Opened at the end of June, this last clay strip was used to tow the *Horsa* gliders recovered in the sector of Ranville, and subsequently re-used in Holland. As for strip B14 at Amblie, it was reserved for the Dakotas for the evacuation of the badly wounded. After Cristot and Ellon, the last British airfield in Normandy became operational at Sainte-Honorine-de-Ducy on August 13.
When the fine weather arrived, enemy number 1 for the pilots was the dust that covered the airfields. Apart from the fact that these dust-clouds provided the Germans with excellent indications and choked up the engines to which suitable filters had not be fitted, worst of all they were the cause of numerous collisions on the strips. From mid-July, in order to cure this plague, the strips were given a good watering each night, with water pumped out of the Seulles, the Mue and the Thue. This arrangement

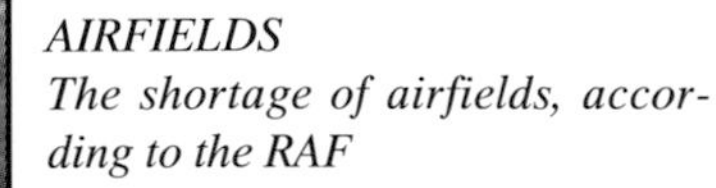

AIRFIELDS
The shortage of airfields, according to the RAF

"The RAF was particularly interested in getting its airfields southeast of Caen. They were mentioned in the plan... but they were not all-important to me. If we won the battle of Normandy, everything else would follow, airfields and all. I wasn't fighting to capture airfields; I was fighting to defeat Rommel in Normandy. This Air Marshal Coningham could scarcely appreciate... he wanted the airfields in order to defeat Rommel, whereas I wanted to defeat Rommel in order, only incidentally, to capture the airfields."

Montgomery

British airfield in the plain of Caen.

had required heavy-duty pumps to be shipped across from England, miles of piping, and the construction of pumping stations on the river banks.

The sappers of the British army were recalled to building sites other than the construction of the airfields. In particular, they were used for stone-quarrying with a view to repairing or consolidating shellholes in the roads, the construction of tank strips or boulevards designed to by-pass built-up areas (the Bayeux by-pass and the Boulevard de la Prairie at Caen) or, finally, to clear up the ruins (Tilly-sur-Seulles, Caen).

Quarrying work by the British.

Carpiquet and the west of Caen

As if the fierce fighting that was taking place on the soil of Normandy was a non-event the outcome of which was in no doubt, the German police in France methodically carried on their task of supplying the camps with deportees. With the complicity of the Vichy authorities, the *Besatzungsmacht* (occupying power) continued, as if it would last for ever, its conscientious job. According to a report of the International Military Tribunal, on July 2 1944, whilst in Normandy the Canadians were preparing to conquer Carpiquet, hardly 150 miles away as the crow flies a train filled with 1,800 deportees left Compiègne for the Reich. It arrived at Dachau via Bremen and Breslau, 60 hours later, with barely 1,200 survivors. The 600 missing deportees had died of thirst or after scuffles that broke out on the journey. Whereas most of France continued breathing the atmosphere of war until mid-August, by that date Bayeux had been a peaceful oasis again for more than two months. There was white bread to eat, *Lucky Strike* cigarettes to smoke and at the soldier's club, the womenfolk of Normandy danced with the officers of the RAF. With scenes of madness on the platforms of Compiègne station, as they embarked onto the goods trains, meanwhile in the plain of Caen, General Keller's 3rd Canadian Division Infantry were attempting to take Carpiquet (Operation *Windsor*) and the western half of the regional capital (Operation *Charnwood).* On July 6, when the deportees from Compiègne at journey's end entered that organized hell, the British were capturing *"die Höhe 112",* after an endless battle, and the Canadians took Carpiquet airfield thirty days behind schedule. To accelerate the capture of Caen by Keller's troops, in the evening of July 7,500 bombers dropped more than 7,000 bombs on the town, already half-destroyed in previous air raids. The next morning another attack took

The Germans' confidence in victory

"There is the certainty that the troops of the Reich are perfectly capable of harrying the enemy, on the day that the supreme command decides to bring in the reserves... None of the German soldiers was afraid on the front. Everywhere you could feel the calm, the assurance, the discipline, the belief in the cause and a kind of detachment." The journalist then gave two instances of the flegmatic attitude prevailing among the front line fighters. The first example was some infantrymen busy defending a house against a violent attack from some British soldiers. "Whilst his comrades were battling away valiantly, one soldier was peacefully cooking an omelette in the ruined kitchen. His main worry was how he was going to get out into the garden to pick some parsley without getting caught in the gunfire." A little further on in the article, there is mention of a brave soldier who while throwing grenades with one hand held a large slice of bread in the other, taking great bites out of it! The journalist added that "these instances would be meaningless but for the fact that they were occurring hundreds and thousands of times over all the way down the firing line! This is how the article ends: "Do we need reminding that a special corps of fighter-pilots has just been formed made up of men whose families have been killed by allied bombs. They have sworn never to land after an air-battle without first shooting down a bomber even if this meant throwing themselves at it!"

L'Illustration

German combat position.
Below: Canadians in the plain of Caen.

place, this time spearheaded by the naval artillery. This was the coup de grâce which was to wipe the beautiful city of Duke William off the map. Only the Saint-Etienne quarter, where big red crosses were displayed, was relatively spared. It was thus an apocalyptic landscape that the Allied troops discovered on entering the town on July 9. In spite of the capture of the part of Caen set on the left bank of the Orne, on July 10, after more than a month of fierce fighting, the Allied bridgehead still lacked depth. Starting just south of Carteret on the west coast of the Cotentin, the front line ended on the Channel, in the region of Cabourg, passing through Carentan, the north of Saint-Lô, Caumont and Caen. The zone in Allied hands represented no more than a tiny spot on a map of France. In a word, results were rather poor and progress was very slow. The enemy resistance was tougher than expected and each offensive was attempted at high cost. The difficulties of the Allies came not from any lack of courage, which is borne out by the fact that between June 6 and mid-July, Rommel lost more than 100,000 men, an average of 2,500 per day, and 225 tanks! No, the inability to make headway denounced by the journalists was rather due to a combination of factors including, though precisely how much it is difficult to

ADMINISTRATION
& REDACTION
34, rue Demolombe
CAEN

ABONNEMENTS
Trois mois : 140 fr.
Six mois : 260 fr.
Un an : 500 fr.
CCP 631-13 - Tél. : 26-36

Le Numéro : 2 Fr.

LIBERTÉ de Normandie

PREMIER QUOTIDIEN RÉGIONAL PARU EN FRANCE LIBÉRÉE

IL Y A UN AN, LE 9 JUILLET 1944...

CAEN, cité martyre, FUT LIBÉRÉE !

say, the bad weather, the hedgerows of the bocage, the technological superiority of the German tanks, the merciless accuracy of the 88-mm guns, the skill of the Germans in gaining advantage from the terrain...

July 14 1944

Excerpt from the message of hope broadcast to the People of Caen by British Foreign Minister Mr Eden for Bastille Day.

"What until now we have been calling the Resistance is not an isolated movement. It has its roots in the soul of the entire French people. It was at Caen, a few days ago, that we were perhaps best able to realize just how much these sentiments are dear to their hearts.

On the first day of the landing, after four years of German occupation the townspeople of this ancient city of Caen had, we might say, had a foretaste of freedom. Nevertheless they had to put up for a whole month with all the weight of the bombing raids by their own allies. After these trials, when we enter the town, the Frenchmen come to meet us with no recriminations: rather, we can read their deep warmth of feeling on their tired faces. Everywhere, quite simply, they go about helping us. Men and women set to work with us. In such circumstances, after such sacrifices, there is no doubt that what we are discovering is the true face of this people.

Now that we we are reconciled in this way, our union is sealed, more forcibly and more solemnly than ever. This union will not only inspire us in the pursuit of the war, it will also enable us to tackle the problems of peace in a spirit of close understanding. On this day, the last July 14, God willing, when the presence of the enemy keeps us apart, I say: Long live France!"

Caen in July 1944.

Caen. The effects of aerial bombings.

"On July 18, a massive bombing raid carried out at dawn by hundreds of planes destroyed villages such as Sannerville and Banneville on the Rouen road and opened up the Bourguebus plateau to the British tanks heading south, and not towards the marshy bocage country to the east. At this date, the point of this movement was no longer liberating Caen, this having already been accomplished by then, but to clear the southern approaches, in the Fleury sector, where several hundreds of thousands of people were still in the quarries, having taken refuge there and been driven out by the Germans around July 14. Moreover the opening of this battlefield changed nothing in the situation along the marshland of the Dives. With the floods, a group of German infantry soldiers held out in the ruins of Troarn until August 19, only 7 miles from Caen at a time when the approach of the tanks was sparking off insurrection in Paris."

Henri Contamine
A civilian's memories
of the Battle for Caen

The Quarries at Fleury-sur-Orne
June-July 1944

Following the violent bombing raids of June 6, then those of July 7, many inhabitants of Caen fled the town in flames. Some pushed a wheelbarrow, others towed a handcart, and they sought refuge in the underground galleries at Fleury-sur-Orne. Sited two miles upstream from Caen, these galleries had been carved out of the foot of the escarpment overhanging the valley of the river Orne, during the quarrying of Caen stone. In the summer of 1944, most of these dark tunnels full of oozing damp had been turned into mushroom beds. According to one witness, some 15,000 to 20,000 people went to live in this cold maze with its slippery floors. The space was fairly soon occupied in organized fashion and a whole community came to life with its old people's quarter, its large families, its police, emergency services with their armbands, its nuns... Each slept either on a mattress or directly on the bed of straw laid out on the ground. A communal kitchen had been set up in a nearby farm. It got its meat supply (up to seven beeves were consumed per day) through groups of volunteers who went out each morning onto the plain to recover and cut up animals killed by shrapnel. During the day, everyone went about their business as usual: collecting wood for the fire, washing clothes and drying them on the bushes, peeling vegetables, commenting on the latest news... The scene made one think of a huge convoy of circus people without the traditional caravans. In this community, whose size varied all the time with the comings and goings, the common behavioural types mixed in all their customary diversity: there were those who started false rumours, those who tried to make themselves useful (helping the sick, the wounded, the old people, volunteering for odd jobs such as fetching supplies, cleaning, going off in search of medical supplies...) The quarries at Fleury were not the only place where there were refugees: others were to be found at the Malherbe grammar school, in underground shelters in cellars, in the abbey of Saint-Etienne and the farms in the villages on the plain of Caen.

THE CANADIANS

Scenes from everyday life

Message to the French people from General Crerar, commander of the 1st Canadian Army

"I just want to say to the French people how happy my soldiers of the Canadian army are to be back on French soil. They have come to fight for freedom on your shores. I ask you to welcome them as brothers-in-arms and as friends. You will find among them soldiers of your own blood, the blood of beautiful Normandy where the battle is now raging. They speak your language. You will also find soldiers of Scottish, English, Irish descent. Together, with you, and our British and American allies, we will defeat the Germans."

> *"Am 17.7 verunglückte der OB der H. Gr. B, Gen. Feldm. Rommel durch einen Autofall." "Marshal Rommel, commander-in-chief of Army Group B, was wounded in a car accident on July 17."*
>
> Official Wehrmacht communiqué on German radio

Goodwood

By mid-July, thanks to the reinforcements that had arrived in the meantime on the beaches or through the artificial harbour, the commanders once again prepared to break out in the sectors of Caen and Saint-Lô. This was the very moment, when the Allies were preparing to regain the operational initiative, that Rommel chose to disappear altogether from Normandy after his car was machine-gunned by a British plane. Three days later, it was Hitler's turn to be the victim of an attempt on his life, in eastern Prussia. This event would not, in fact, make much difference to the situation on the Western front. It was in this context that, on July 18, the British units launched their second outflanking operation around Caen, this time on the eastern flank (Operation *Goodwood)*. Reserves mustered in the half-circle going from the river Dives and comprising the eastern end of the beachhead were gigantic. With three armoured divisions, 700 guns and 2,000 bombers overhead, *Goodwood* remains the most massive operation of the entire Normandy campaign. After *"der Fall von Caen"* (the fall of Caen), on July 18, in spite of the scale of resources deployed, the southward thrust at the German positions was soon held up on the outskirts of the Lower Norman capital. Montgomery's disappointment was counterbalanced by the certainty that once again he had forced the enemy to use his tank reserves. A month later, at the final showdown near Falaise, the British general had the satisfaction of reaping the benefits of his plug-away policy.

Flail tank, specialized in clearing minefields.

Colombelles. Bombing the steelworks. The canal from Caen to the sea can be made out to the far right.

Last report of the situation on the Normandy front by Rommel forwarded to Hitler by Marshal von Kluge (July 15 1944)

In this report which reads like an ultimatum, Rommel begs Hitler to draw the political consequences from the German defeat in Normandy. In other words, he demands that some agreement be reached with the western Allies.

"Die Lage an der Front der Normandie... The situation on the Normandy front is becoming each day more and more difficult, it is heading towards an acute crisis... Within a measurable time, the enemy will succeed in breaking through our thinly held front, and in thrusting deep into France. The consequences of this will be unavoidable. The force is fighting heroically everywhere but the "ungleiche Kampf" (unequal struggle) is nearing its end. In my opinion, it is necessary to draw the appropriate conclusion from this situation. It is my duty as Army Group commander to make this position clear to you."

THE BRITISH

Scenes from everyday life

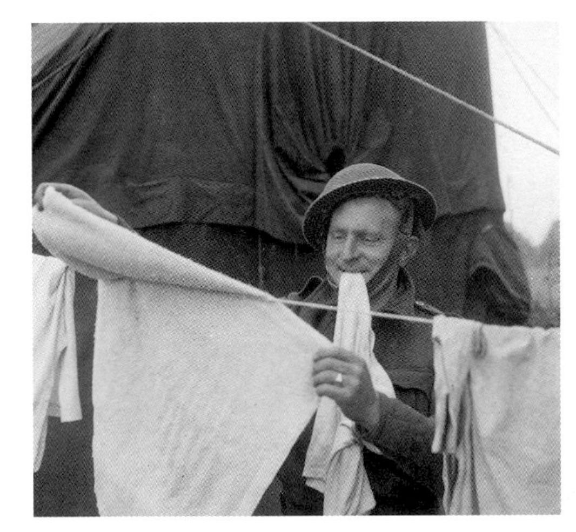

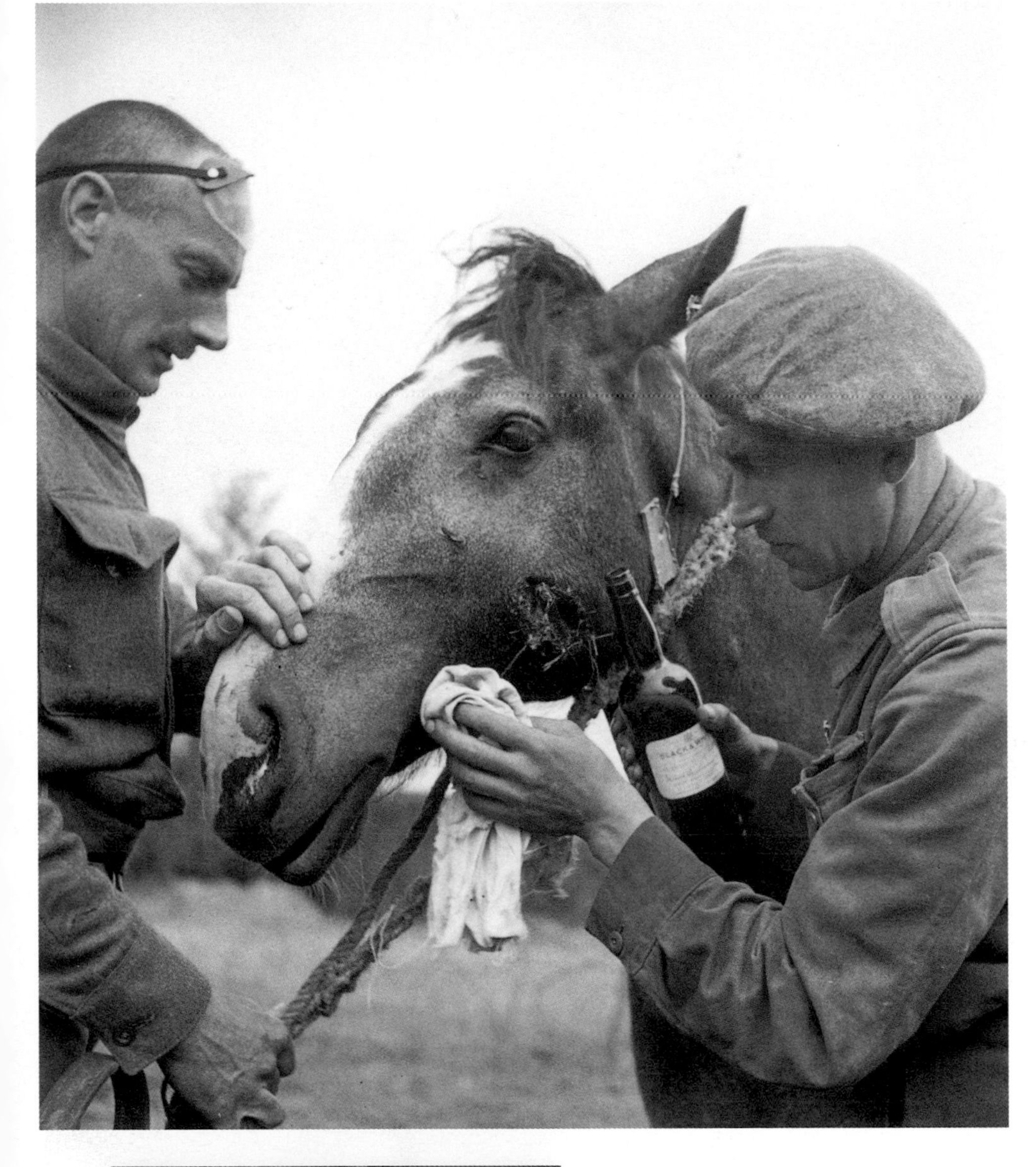

Life for the British soldier

"Egg-hunting was the only available sport at Sainte-Honorine which the garrison engaged in... The hens certainly did look harassed. The great idea was to discover a half-dozen of them that were used to going and laying further away from the rest, in a quiet corner, then drop in on them three or four times each morning. That way you got three eggs a day. Otherwise you had to chase a hen around the hen-coop and sit it out until it laid an egg... So we would poke around in the ruins and all show silly delight when we fared better than usual. There were strawberries in the mayor's garden, but they were reserved for the early birds. These little nothings gave us some slight impression of what it would be like to be at home."

E. Belfield and H. Essame

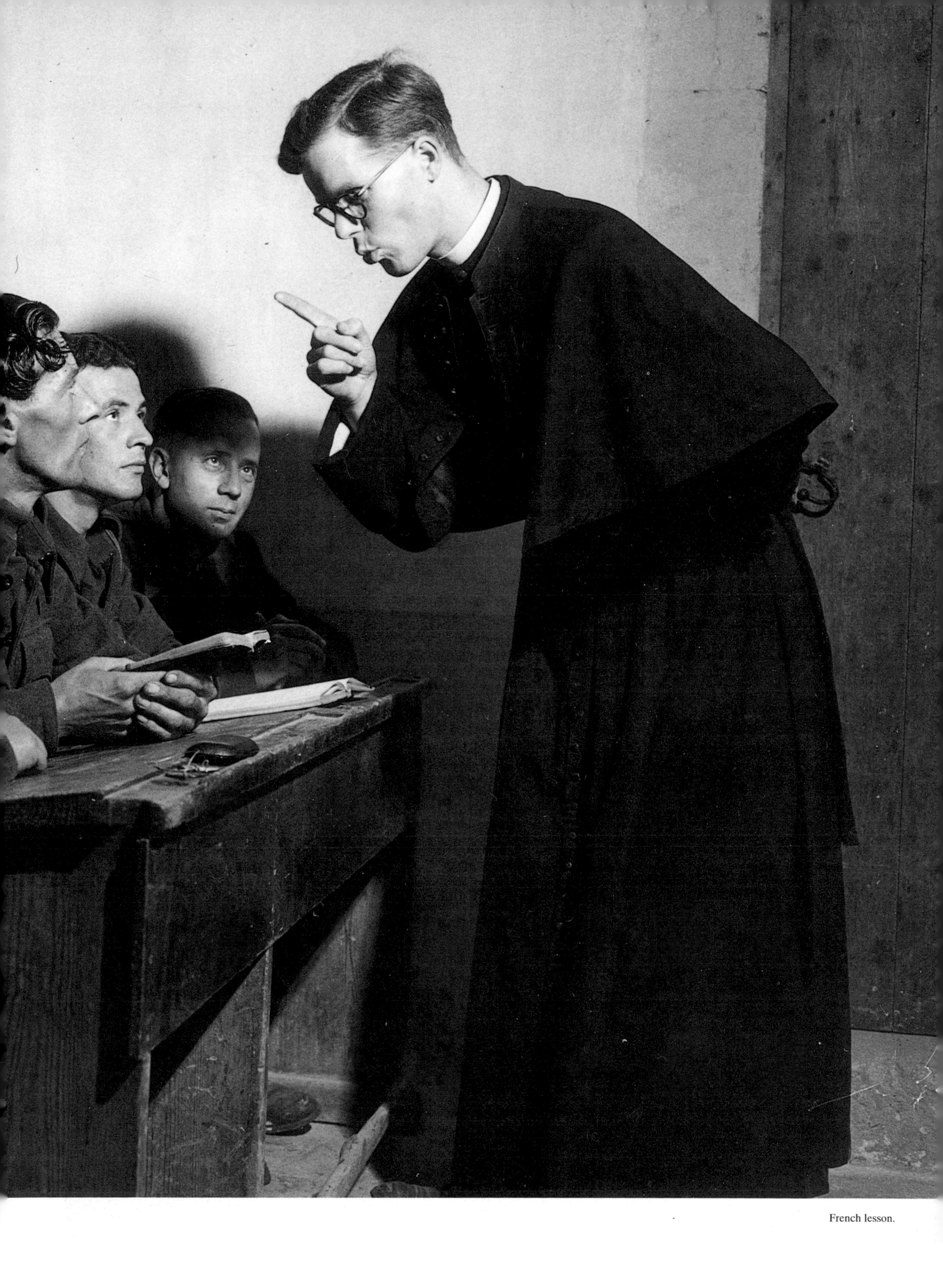

French lesson.

SAINT-LÔ

The Americans in the area around St-Lô.

What is more, in drawing the enemy forces once again onto the eastern flank, Montgomery facilitated Bradley's operation in the sector of Saint-Lô. After a month of making no headway in the bocage, the important crossroads and rail junction of Saint-Lô was captured, like Caen, after a great deal of murderous combat. By July 20, the Americans had lost 62,000 men including 10,000 killed since the start of the campaign, and the British 35,000 including 6,000 killed.

Saint-Lô. The station.

Saint-Lô. Aerial view (USAF).

"In the evening, the flying fortresses drop their bombs all around us, concentrating mainly on the sidings at Airel and Lison, Pont-Hébert and Saint-Lô. We set up our poor camp as best we can for the night. Unable to sleep, we say the rosary over and over again. Towards midnight, wave after wave of flying fortresses thunder over our heads... Where are they going? ... Alas, to the unfortunate town of Saint-Lô...

At ten past midnight, a dreadful din fills the whole town with fear, shaken to its very foundations. For twenty minutes the bombs fell all around at a rate of one per second, and the ensuing fires would only make matters worse.

Some survivors who had been walking all night arrived at dawn. The same story was on everyone's lips: "Saint-Lô has been completely destroyed, the streets are no more than a pile of ruins. The north tower of Notre-Dame has collapsed, and the top of the other tower has been smashed. The prefect's residence is on fire; in the workroom, two nuns and several children are buried under the rubble. The hospital has also been hit, but fortunately the nuns and the sick have taken shelter under the rock at la Poterne".

Abbé Bertot

First café reopened at Saint-Lô.

Cobra

If *Goodwood* was a fiasco, on the other hand, *Cobra,* codename of the break-out undertaken by the Americans from July 25, was a stupendous success. Preceded by an exceptionally powerful preparatory air strike, Cobra opened the breach and led the Americans into Coutances on July 28, then Granville and Avranches, on July 31. Finally, after 55 days of fighting, the moment so long awaited by Eisenhower and the whole world had come: the western flank of the German defences collapsed. Ignoring the suffering of the men and the losses which, since June 6, had risen to almost 130,000 soldiers and 250 tanks, Hitler ordered Rommel's successor von Kluge, to make the most of the over-deployment of the US forces and advance towards Avranches to cut off the units that had unwisely ventured into Brittany.

Granville, July 1944.

US Air Force formation flying over the Cotentin.

Return from a mission.

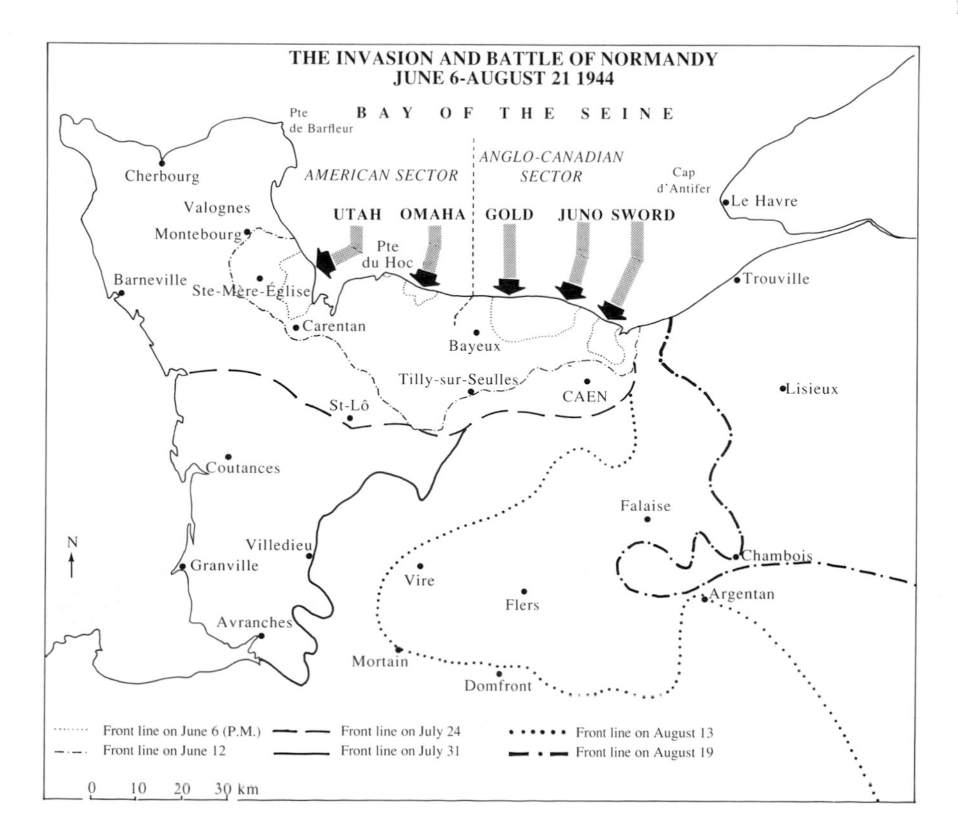

Normandy and the Normans as seen by the Americans (February 1944)

Before embarking on the cross-Channel invasion operation, the chiefs-of-staff of 1st US Army had accumulated a vast amount of documentation on relief and hydrography as well as road and port facilities in Normandy. Here are a few excerpts from the various reports contained in the 1st American Army archives. These documents were updated from time to time, and are interesting because they show how the American military saw the Normandy region and its inhabitants. The first text deals with hygiene and the second with the probable attitude of the local population.

“Public health in Normandy leaves something to be desired, although for the time being there is no epidemic in the region. It must be remembered that an epidemic is always to be feared whenever there is a heavy concentration of men in the same place (for instance typhus is rampant in a POW camp). Water should be used with caution: the natives drink and cook with untreated water although, at the same time, they use excrement as fertilizer, which naturally produces pollution of the soil and the water table. In Normandy and more generally in the north-west of France, there are mosquitoes but they do not pass on disease. On the other hand, the flies that exist in large numbers in the pig-sties, byres and milk-parlors do carry enteritis. In the same line of thought, an invasion of lice has to be reported due to reduced resistance among the population, the lack of hygiene (no soap, no hot water, no anti-lice cream). These parasites which transmit fever are easy enough to fight off with DDT. Fleas are also common, as are ticks, moths, cockroaches, rats and wasps in summer. In Normandy, impetigo, scabies, dermatosis and intestinal infections (diarrhea and gastro-enteritis) are especially common owing to the water pollution, the absence of pasteurized milk products and the general lack of hygiene. It must be realized that the German soldiers have come back from Africa with various intestinal complaints and that on the continent there is an upsurge of venereal disease (syphilis, gonorrhea). It is therefore recommanded that condoms be used. However, the disease to be feared most is tuberculosis. It is estimated that 1,5 million persons in France currently carry the disease. Then come diphtheria, meningitis and smallpox (63 cases were notified France during 1942). We should therefore arrange to have the troops vaccinated and accustom the men to maintain the highest possible levels of personal hygiene and that begins with dealing with parasites”.

"Even in their own country, the people of Normandy are held to be difficult to get to know. Most of them are politically rather conservative countryfolk, apart from some working class populations in the ports of Cherbourg and Le Havre. The collaborationist parties are implanted in Normandy but have relatively few active members. Doriot’s PPF who sympathize with the new Order has a local branch at Caen. Its main recruitment base is the popular classes. Deat’s RNP which also warmly defended collaboration with Germany recruits most of its members among the intellectuals from the PSF (Parti Social Français) or the Croix de Feu. The majority of the people of Normandy are anti-German and anti-Vichy, but that does not necessarily mean they will be pro-American or pro-British, once the liberation comes. At the time of the invasion, a small group of brave resistants and anti-nazis can be counted on to assist us. The rest of the population will wait until it is quite clear that the operation has succeeded before joining us. it must be realized that the attitude of the Normans will depend on the losses that they will have sustained during the preliminary air raids and also on the conduct of the invading troops. If we are to win over the local population a minimum of control will have to be used which giving them a hand to repair the damage. There is likely to be tension if most of their hopes as to improved supplies and work and greater freedom are not fulfilled. In fact, the enthusiasm of the people of Normandy for the Anglo-American forces will be inversely proportional to the time that we occupy their province. We must also remember that bad feeling is to be expected between patriots and collaborationists, moreover a power struggle is likely between the different resistance groups. Informers are also likely to come forward. All these things could create problems for us. No acts of sabotage against our military installations are likely to be committed by the French. Any elements that have got closely involved with the Germans will probably have fled before we get to them. The danger of sabotage committed by the enemy behind our lines must not be under-estimated. We must keep a close eye on the former workers for the Todt Organization as well as on former members of fascist organizations such as Darnand’s Milice, the Fascists’ Corps Franc and the Legion Nationale Populaire of Deat’s RNP."

After a short period immediately after the invasion when they were on their guard and reserved, we read in the American archives that the Normans became friendly and cooperative. Unfortunately, adds the intelligence officer, any exchanges would remain limited because of the language barrier.

US 1st Army Report

THE AMERICANS

Scenes from everyday life

The military tribunal and American soldiers in Normandy

"A few days after the invasion, a military tribunal was set up in the American sector. Initially housed at Vierville, it was later moved to Isigny town hall. This tribunal was responsible for trying civilian suspects. Between June 12 and August 1, 223 individuals came up for trial. Among them, there were about ten enemy agents, seventy others who were sufficiently dangerous to be handed over to the French authorities for internment. The rest were either small-time collaborationists or German soldiers who had deserted in civilian clothing. The spies and suspicious individuals who worked for the Germans nearly all belonged to some collaborationist party or were young Frenchmen who, in order to avoid being requisitioned for compulsory labour service in Germany, had accepted to enter service for the occupying forces. Originally, these traitors had been recruited to help fight the maquisards, after the invasion, the German authorities had had them retrained as spies and saboteurs. For their destructive actions they used British equipment that had been dropped by parachute for the Resistance and intercepted by the Germans. The Military Police also had to intervene to ban the opening of a brothel at Isigny, aimed primarily at the American soldiers. Apart from these few exceptions, the military tribunal's principal task was to try cases of misconduct among the American soldiers (non-regulation uniforms, infringements of the highway code...). A special section was responsible for more serious offences (rape, theft, murder, looting, unlawful slaughter of animals. ..).
Between June 12 and August 1, according to 1st US Army reports, the tribunal had to try difficult 117 cases including 22 cases of looting, 17 acts of sexual violence, 25 cases of rape or attempted rape, 10 cases of animal slaughter and as many instances of misuse of fire-arms. To this list must be added house-breaking, various petty thefts, civilian car thefts or the theft of state owned property, one case of buggery and the unexplained death of an American soldier... Fifty American soldiers including forty-nine blacks were tried for rape or attempted rape."

La Presse
PARIS

The military cemeteries

Evacuating the wounded.

The American army had special units responsible for burying soldiers who had been killed on the field of battle. At Omaha beach, it was 607th Grave Record Company that was assigned the task of finding a suitable place for gathering together the bodies of the soldiers killed on the beach and a site for setting up a provisional cemetery according to standard specifications, avoiding marshland and earth that was too hard to dig. Equipped with bulldozers, this unit would look after digging the trenches (at least 5 feet deep as per instructions) and carried out an accurate count of the graves. At Omaha, the first cemetery was set up at Saint Laurent-sur-Mer. Later other burial grounds were opened, in particular at La Cambe (graves of the soldiers of 29th Infantry Division), Pouppeville (365 graves), Sainte-Mère-Eglise for the 3,213 soldiers of the 9th US Division killed on French soil, at Orglandes, Blosville for 330 paratroopers of 82nd Airborne and at Hiesville for 101st Airborne. At the end of July, a new cemetery was opened at Marigny.

In the sector of 1st US Army, approximately 700 soldiers were allocated to cemetery duty assisted, from June 8, by an equal number of German prisoners employed in digging the graves. The American command also made use of civilian labour, in particular for decorating and looking after the cemeteries. Each soldier was interred in a special shroud with his identity disc. If none had been found, in order to establish the soldier's identity at a later date, fingerprints were taken of both hands, as were his weight, height, colour of hair, birthmarks (scars, beauty spots, malformations) and the arrangement of the teeth including crowns, bridges, and missing teeth...). Uniform white crosses were used to mark the graves, or a star of David if the deceased was of Jewish religion.

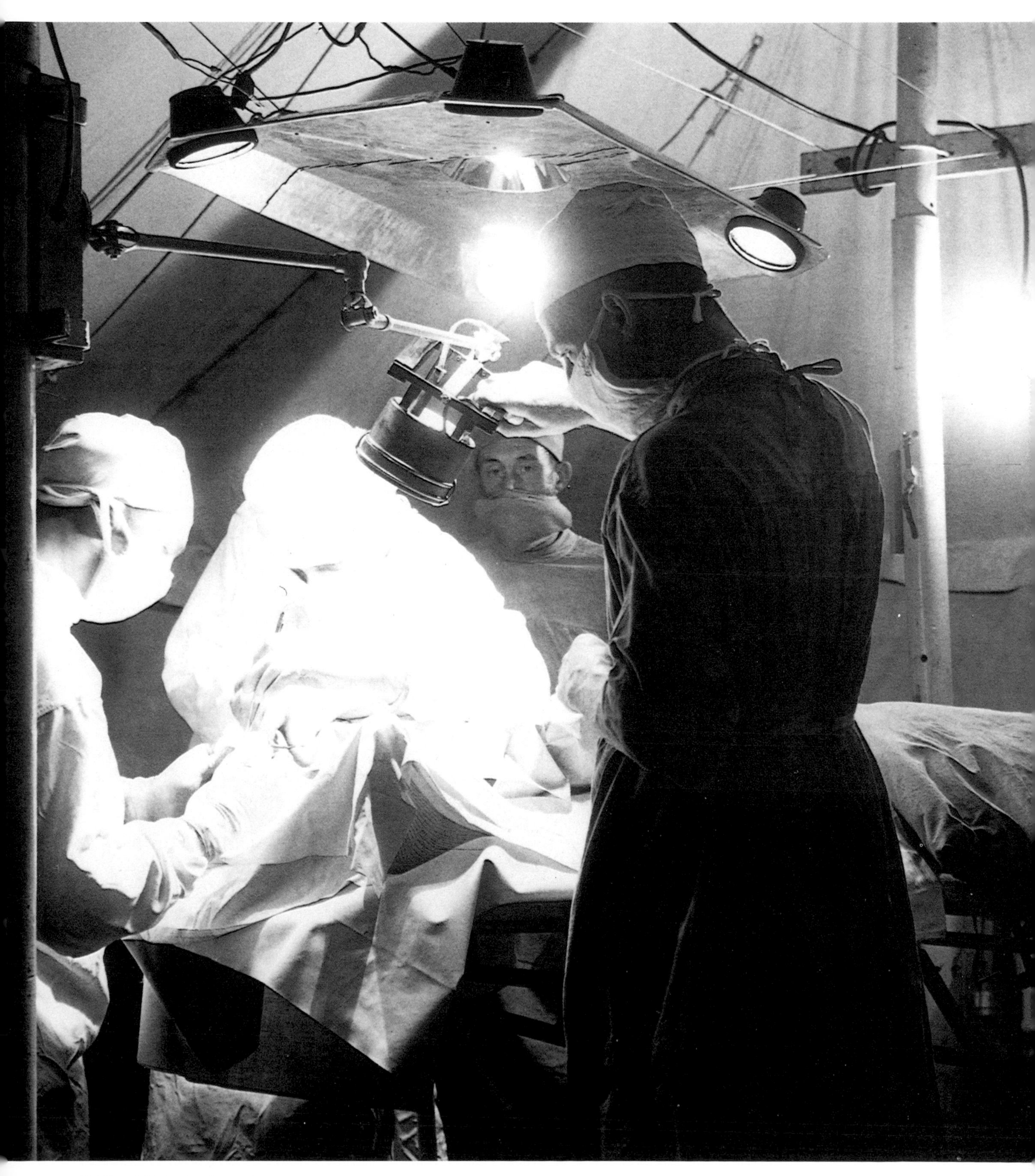

Field hospital in the American sector.

AVRANCHES August 1944

At the beginning of August, the American forces deployed over more than 80 miles between Cherbourg and Pontaubault at the gateway to Brittany, with a relatively thin flank on a level with Avranches. This vulnerable sector did not go unnoticed by Hitler, who ordered General von Kluge to launch a mainly tank counter-offensive westwards from the region of Mortain, i.e. in the direction of the Bay of the Mont Saint Michel. The aim of the operation was to cut the US forces in two and to isolate in the Brittany peninsula the units that had been unwisely committed there. It was indeed a unique opportunity and an extremely tempting gamble. Fore-warned of enemy intentions by his wire-tapping department who had decoded the wireless messages, Bradley was on his guard and had guns at the ready. Launched in the fog in the early hours of August 7, with the help of half a dozen armoured divisions, or roughly 400 *Panzers, Lüttich,* codename of the large-scale operation organized down to the smallest details by Hitler, was blocked the very same day. Equipped with anti-tank rockets placed under the wings, the *Jabos* (as the German soldiers called the Allied fighter-bombers), had worked wonders. Once again, the enemy had wasted about fifty tanks in a risky not to say desperate operation due to the lack of adequate air cover. As von Kluge wrote to Hitler a few hours before committing suicide, the *Angriff* (the attack) in the direction of Avranches against 1st US Army had been impossible to execute and had not the slightest chance of succeeding. Doomed almost from the outset, Operation *Lüttich* was to be the Germans' final effort in Normandy before they withdrew.

Avranches, at the end of July 1944.

FALAISE August 1944

Meanwhile on the other flank, Montgomery launched Operation *Totalize* in the Caen sector on the evening of August 7. Assigned to the 1st Canadian Army, the aim of this offensive was to break out southwards through the enemy lines. As it turned out, after several days of fierce fighting, the impetus of the Canadians, with temporary support from a Polish armoured division, was broken and the undertaking tailed off about fifteen miles outside Falaise. Without wasting any time, a second tank offensive was launched. Codenamed *Tractable,* this new thrust had the same objective as before: to break through the German positions blocking the route to Falaise. Four days after *Tractable* was launched, that is on August 18, the Anglo-Canadian troops finally prised open the gates to the town.

Tracks left by tanks in the plain of Caen.

German vehicle after being machine-gunned by a Jabo.
Opposite: an armoured column heading for Falaise.

US bomber over Domfront.
Following page: an aerial view of Falaise after the aerial bombardment.

While these military events were taking place, the American armed forces were pursuing their victorious advance in Brittany whilst another section headed off towards the Loire. After liberating Rennes and Le Mans, the US units headed off straight towards the Seine and Paris, joined by 2nd French Armoured Division under General Leclerc, who had landed early in August at Utah Beach. There was no more time to be lost. When Montgomery, after two months of vain attempts, finally broke through the enemy's defensive positions south of Caen and started bringing heavy pressure to bear in the direction of Falaise, the American prepared to attack the German armies from behind. The two jaws of the pincer drew inexorably closer and closer. However, in spite of the Allied efforts, the *Falaise Gap,* sealed at Chambois in the evening of August 19 after the Canadians and the Americans had met, was not carried out with as promptly as it should have been. A sizable portion, maybe as much as half of the German forces had made their escape and crossed the Seine, in spite of the destruction of the bridges. The battle for Normandy was definitively over two days later, on August 21 in a farmyard at Tournai-on-Dives when fifty thousand men comprising all that remained of the two big German formations that had fought against the Allies in Normandy during the summer of 1944, were captured in the pocket.

Pursuing their onward march with 2nd French Armoured

German motorcyclists in the Livarot sector.

American convoys moving up towards Chambois.

A bomber in flames after a forced landing.

"In this ring of fire that the airforce covers with bombs, in this battle of the nations where sometimes personal revenge stimulates people to greater bravery, in the merciless combat between small units, life is hell. The inhabitants flee across the fields or seek the shelter of their trenches and cellars. Occasionally they get killed in their homes when a tank backs into the wall and knocks it over, as happened to one family in Chambois."

R. Mouton

Battle scenes around Tournai-sur-Dives.

in the lead, the Allies entered Paris on August 24. With the crossing of the Seine on one side and the Loire on the other, the *Overlord* plan launched on June 6 was completely achieved. Thus at the end of August (D+87), Eisenhower could once again rub his hands: he had accomplished the first part of his mission in North-West Europe three days ahead of schedule as laid out in London in the spring of 1944. Another campaign was beginning, the campaign for the liberation of France, with *Dragoon,* the landing on the shores of Provence carried out by Franco-American forces on August 15 1944, marking its first stage. The big showdown in Normandy had been a murderous one for both sides. By August 31, Allied losses had reached the figure of 37,000 killed (an average of 400 per day since June 6), 153,000 wounded and 20,000 missing (mostly prisoners), giving an overall total of a little over 200,000 men. On the other side, according to the archives, the *Wehrmacht* had lost approximately 300,000 men, an average of 3,500 per day. The figure for tank losses, again according to *Wehrmacht* archives, was roughly 800 *Panzers,* or ten a day. Although a decisive event in the Second World War, the battle of Normandy did not bring an end to the conflict. Another 8 months of hard fighting was to follow after *der Kessel von Falaise* (the Falaise Gap) before the 3rd Reich would capitulate unconditionally. However, as Colonel Stacey, the Canadian army's official historian, points out, in Normandy a death blow had been administered to the morale of the German army. This time there is no doubt about it: Falaise was indeed the beginning of the end.

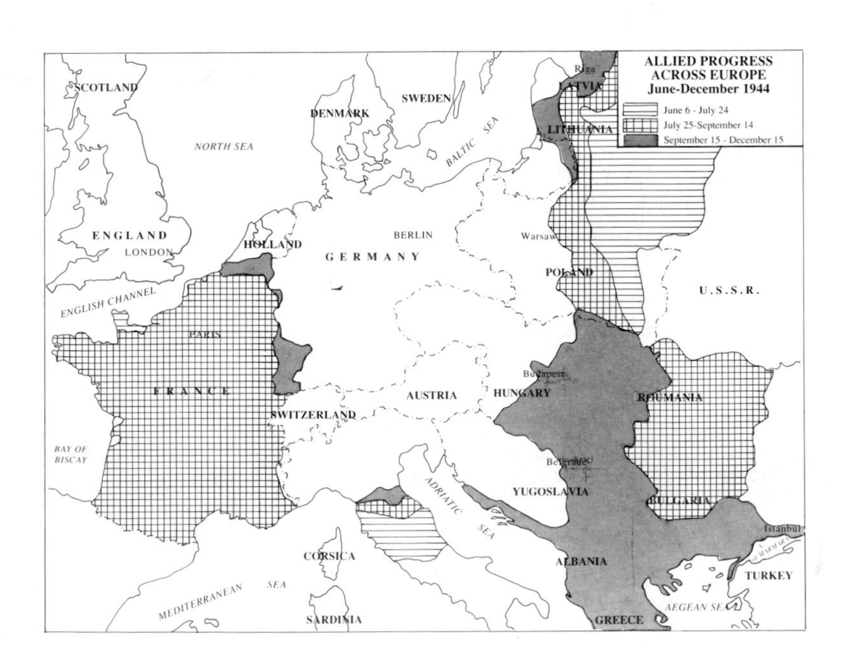

The Canadians rejoice after the closing of the pocket.

THE PRISONERS OF WAR

On D Day, POW camps were set up on the edge of the beaches. Later a large camp for 10,000 prisoners was opened in the American sector, at Foucarville, followed by another, a few days later, at Valognes. At the end of June, a third big camp was set up at Formigny (to the rear of *Omaha Beach*), then, as the advance progressed, two new camps were opened, one at Saint-Jean-de-Daye and the other at Saint-Jores (at the end of July).

By mid-June, in the 1st Army sectors, the Americans had taken a little over 3,000 prisoners. A fortnight later, after Cherbourg had fallen, the number was in excess of 40,000 and had passed the 60,000 mark by the end of July, at the time of the break-out at Avranches. Out of this total, 55,000 POWs were sent to Britain on board LSTs (the remaining 5,000 were the badly wounded). Apart from digging graves, the prisoners of war were employed on a rota basis by the health service of the American armies (setting up field hospitals). All superior officers of the *Wehrmacht* captured were interrogated by the G2 (intelligence officer in the US army). Later on, in order to dispose of material for writing as objectively as possible the official history of the American army during the Second World War, the US Army History Department would ask all high-ranking German military either to answer their questions or more often to produce a written report on their military activities during the war. Thus we now possess a collection of several thousand reports from the commanders of a defeated army and covering a wide range of topics.

SAFE CONDUCT

The German soldier who carries this safe-conduct is using it as a sign of his genuine wish to give himself up. He is to be disarmed, to be well looked after, to receive food and medical attention as required, and is to be removed from the danger zone as soon as possible.

PASSIERSCHEIN

An die britischen und amerikanischen Vorposten: Der deutsche Soldat, der diesen Passierschein vorzeigt, benutzt ihn als Zeichen seines ehrlichen Willens, sich zu ergeben. Er ist zu entwaffnen. Er muss gut behandelt werden. Er hat Anspruch auf Verpflegung und, wenn nötig, ärztliche Behandlung. Er wird so bald wie möglich aus der Gefahrenzone entfernt.

Tract inviting German soldiers to surrender.

Photograph used by Allied propaganda to show that even the Hitler Youth could be made to surrender.

After the liberation, the prisoners were employed in mineclearing.

Prisoner-of-war camp.

German prisoners landing on a British beach.

An old Norman couple offering a simple bunch of flowers picked from the garden hedge to a young American soldier killed on the side of a road to Cherbourg.

PHOTOGRAPHIC CREDITS
PUBLIC ARCHIVES, Ottawa - BUNDESARCHIV, Koblenz - IMPERIAL WAR MUSEUM, London - MEMORIAL, Caen - NATIONAL ARCHIVES, Washington - Cover photo: Claire SABLERY

CONTENTS

Printed in France by the Mame printing press, Tours (37)
I.S.B.N. : 2.7373.1287.6 - Dépôt légal : juin 1993 - N° éditeur : 2626.01.05.06.93